"Through my years of counseling, I've discovered that comparison is a trap ensnaring many women. Social media only reinforces the idea that 'other wives' or 'other moms' are smarter, prettier, happier, and more accomplished. Donna Gibbs is a Christian counselor who understands this devastating struggle, and in her excellent book she offers encouraging, practical, biblical guidance to help readers find their way back to peace, wholeness, and security as women made in God's image."

Dr. Greg Smalley, vice president,
Marriage and Family Formation, Focus on the Family

"Love this book! I'm in a very competitive environment where looks and comparisons play a huge role in being successful and 'making it,' causing us to see ourselves in a way God never intended but, unfortunately, happens to many of us. It's easy to get held back by insecurities, anxiety, and fear. Donna gives us real, practical tools to help us not let 'the thief' steal our joy of who God created each of us to be."

Meghan Woods, Nashville recording artist

"Insecurity keeps many women from reaching their potential. In her counseling ministry, Donna Gibbs has helped many women find freedom to explore the future unafraid. Now, in this book, she shares those insights in a practical, readable format. All readers will profit from these insights."

Gary D. Chapman, PhD, author of *The Five Love Languages*

"God uses Donna in this book to unpack, clarify, and provide a pathway for healing one of the most important considerations of who we are as humans—our identity."

Kevin Wimbish, MS, LMFT; licensed marriage
and family therapist; director, Family Life Coach

"*Silencing Insecurity* beautifully and poignantly touches on the many aspects of life that plague women in America. The comparisons, the struggles, the falling short, and the unrealistic expectations paralyze and restrict women as they mature in this competitive social-media era. Donna Gibbs, a therapist with much wisdom and the experience of thousands of hours of counseling, has had a bird's-eye view of clients' hearts and struggles. She pushes in probing the effects of the difficult hurts and wounds so many endure. But she provides hope as well! As a Christian counselor for thirty years myself, I know there is sacredness in hearing of the inner workings of people's lives and relationships. We're all struggling. *Silencing Insecurity* does a superb job of hitting the panoply of issues that plague us all."

Dee Jones Adams, PhD, Certified EFT Therapist, director of Baton Rouge Christian Counseling Center

SILENCING INSECURITY

Also by Donna Gibbs

Becoming Resilient: How to Move through
Suffering and Come Back Stronger

SILENCING
INSECURITY

BELIEVING GOD'S TRUTH
ABOUT YOU

DONNA GIBBS

Revell

a division of Baker Publishing Group
Grand Rapids, Michigan

Published by Revell
a division of Baker Publishing Group
PO Box 6287, Grand Rapids, MI 49516-6287
www.revellbooks.com

Printed in the United States of America

Library of Congress Cataloging-in-Publication Data
Names: Gibbs, Donna, 1972– author.
Title: Silencing insecurity : believing God's truth about you / Donna Gibbs.
Description: Grand Rapids : Revell-Baker Publishing Group, 2018. | Includes
    bibliographical references and index.
Identifiers: LCCN 2018014411 | ISBN 9780800729820 (pbk. : alk. paper)
Subjects: LCSH: Christian women—Religious life. | Trust in God—Christianity. |
    Identity (Psychology)—Religious aspects—Christianity.
Classification: LCC BV4527 .G525 2018 | DDC 248.8/43—dc23
LC record available at https://lccn.loc.gov/2018014411

Some of the names and details of the people and situations described in this book have been changed or presented in composite form in order to ensure the privacy of those with whom the author has worked.

18 19 20 21 22 23 24   7 6 5 4 3 2 1

Dedicated to all who are seeking freedom.
May you find hope and healing here.

Contents

Acknowledgments

I would like to thank Janet Dohm, who introduced me to Jesus when I was a teenager. Who knows the lives that have been changed as a result of your genuine enthusiasm in sharing the truth and then following through with discipleship. Your pouring into my teenage life made a difference!

Where Janet left off, Sam and Nell Bailey stepped in, discipling me and hundreds of other young men and women during our college years. Made-from-scratch meals in your home, worship on your back porch, and some of the most inspiring and enthusiastic teachings I've ever heard. Many leaders in ministry have been born out of your hearts and your home. I trust you will be eternally blessed by the difference you made in our lives.

To my husband, Mark, who reminds me daily that I am his princess. Thank you for cheering me on. I love you!

And to Vicki Crumpton, Amy Ballor, Jennifer Nutter, Patti Brinks, Erin Bartels, Brianne Dekker, Arielle Wade, Adam Lorenz, and the entire Revell team, thank you once again for your partnership and dedication to the work of building up the body of Christ. Your efforts behind the scenes have eternal significance.

Introduction

I felt a sense of vulnerability and a rage of anger unlike anything I had ever experienced. My wallet had been stolen and the offender was using my identity for his own good pleasures. I had been robbed. I felt defenseless and violated. If only I had known a thief had been lurking, I would have been more careful. I would have kept my guard up and been more alert. But now, it was too late. The damage was done. I'd been betrayed by an unknown enemy, and the destruction was to my credit, my pride, and my overall sense of security.

Millions of people fall victim to identity theft every year. The majority of those victims have no idea they have been targeted until months, or even years, after the crime. But I want to talk to you about an even more common, subtler, and more dangerous form of identity theft that is claiming unsuspecting victims. It is the theft of our purpose, our joy, our stability, and our very being. Webster defines *identity crisis* as "personal, psychosocial conflict especially in adolescence that involves confusion about one's social role and often a sense of loss of continuity to one's personality."[1] Unfortunately, I know only a few individuals whose "psychosocial conflict" ended in adolescence. In fact, many women at every stage and circumstance in life continue to be just as conflicted as they were in adolescence. What about you? Are you secure in who you are? Or do you still feel like a teenager who is tossed to and fro by each passing circumstance? If this describes you, then you will likely relate to some of the testimonies below.

"I don't know what to do with myself now that my children are out of the home. Who am I if not a mother?"

"When my husband left me, he took part of me with him. He was my everything."

"I just finished college and everyone says I have great potential. Yet I am still trying to find myself, and I truly have no idea who I really am."

"I take care of my husband and constantly run around taking care of the kids. I think I have lost myself in the midst of caring for everyone else."

"My husband struggles with an addiction to pornography. Clearly I am not good enough or attractive enough. This is my fault."

"I was abused as a young child. I've spent my life believing I am dirty and deserving of what happened to me."

"My physical condition has gotten worse, and I can't do the things I once could. I feel so inadequate."

"I work so hard to keep everyone happy, and I hate conflict. I lose sleep if I learn someone is disappointed in me."

"If only I had a boyfriend, I would feel better about myself. I feel so anxious and dejected when I don't have someone special in my life."

"My past prevents me from having a future. I don't expect to ever be able to experience happiness."

"I seem to fail at most everything I do. Why should I even risk trying?"

"If only I were thinner . . ."

"If only I were smarter . . ."

"If only I were younger . . ."

"I feel inadequate."

"I feel worthless."

If you have ever struggled with thoughts or emotions like these, then you have been the target of identity theft. Unfortunately, you are not alone. So, join with your sisters, and let's enter a journey that is mysterious but also freeing. Let's get to know our "thieves," those areas that trap us and leave us vulnerable to feelings of inadequacy. We're living in a society surrounded by thieves, so we need to be prepared, don't you think?

After we expose those thieves, we will uncover the problems they leave behind. Boy, can they make some messes. Next, we're going to look at an individual in Scripture who got into some messes of her own because of her lurking thieves.

Thankfully, God always provides a way out. And we're going to discover the path out of insecurity through the Formula for Wholeness. This formula will connect the destructive thoughts, emotions, and behaviors that are keeping us stuck in a pit of insecurity. We'll also be encouraged by some biblical characters who outsmarted their insecurities and exemplified a life of wholeness. We're going to investigate how they succeeded and pray that God will give us the grace and courage to apply the same principles. That journey will be a breath of fresh air.

If you have picked up this book because you struggle with insecurities, I want to give you a word of hope. You don't have to live the rest of your life feeling that you don't measure up. You don't have to settle for living as if you aren't enough. You don't have to settle for living with the emotional instability that results from insecurities. You don't have to settle for the relational chaos, indecisiveness, and unnecessary suffering invited by an inaccurate belief system regarding yourself. *It's time to stop the theft of your identity and gain stability through rescuing the significance of the person you were created to be.* It's time to experience freedom from your insecurities.

When you finish this journey, I am confident you will be able to more accurately identify the thieves that plague your identity. More importantly, you will have all the tools you'll ever need to completely disarm those thieves and gain back the security that never should have been stolen. *Let's get this rescue mission started!*

Donna

PART 1

IDENTITY THIEVES

A thief will use any trick to deceive us. Take, for instance, the thieves who try to steal our personal information. If they can trick us out of the right details, they can steal our financial worth. But there are other, subtler threats to our personal identity.

We look to various people or things to affirm our value. These can be positive, such as our appearance or our success, our background or our life experiences, our relationships or our church involvement. Sometimes the things that influence our perceived value are not good things and instead are painful experiences of rejection or even previous trauma. The first part of this book will cover the typical things that impact our sense of identity. When our sense of self, our perceived worth, is overly attached or perhaps dependent on these external things, they can become thieves that steal from us, robbing us of joy and contentment. The things that influence how we feel are in and of themselves not problematic. Being pretty or successful, for instance, are not problems unless our security depends too much on our appearance or performance. By the end of this section, you will know with certainty whether your security has secretly and destructively been stolen by one of these thieves.

We'll conclude this section with an investigation of the chief thief—Satan—and his desire to steal a stable, healthy, and secure identity from you and from me.

1

Appearance and Comparisons

You probably remember the popular TV series *American Idol*. I had the rare opportunity one season to join a young girl in her audition. You've never seen so many alterations to bodily appearances in one place in your life. The startling personalities, styles, accessories, and painted-on faces screamed, "Notice me! Please notice me!" You expect this kind of parade at auditions for a reality TV show, but down deep in our hearts, we're *all* screaming, "Notice me. *Please* notice me." Without a secure identity, we either go to drastic measures to gain attention so that we can feel a semblance of peace with ourselves or withdraw into feelings of inadequacy, convinced that we just don't really matter. The good news is that a secure identity is within reach of everyone, even you and me.

You are probably not flamboyantly presenting yourself to judges at a voice competition, but is it possible you are still vulnerable to the thief of appearance and comparisons? Let's consider a few questions that might reveal the answer.

1. Have you ever changed your outfit repeatedly before you headed out the door?
2. Have you had thoughts that you weren't pretty enough?
3. Are you a chronic dieter, or have you ever been vulnerable to an eating disorder?
4. Are there some aspects of your appearance that you find disgusting?
5. Do a few pounds or clothing sizes have the power to significantly inflate or deflate your self-confidence?
6. Have you given up on taking care of yourself physically because ultimately you believe that you don't measure up?
7. Do you obsess over compliments or criticisms you receive regarding your appearance?
8. Do you often compare your appearance to others?
9. Have you ever behaved a little oddly with hopes of gaining attention?
10. Have you avoided situations or people altogether because you felt you didn't measure up?

If you answered yes to any of these questions, then consider the cause. Tell the truth. It's just me and you—and I think I might already know the answer. Why did you do those things? What thoughts were going through your mind about yourself? What emotions were you experiencing? I have a feeling I know, because I have done a few of those frantic dances myself. We did these things because we were self-conscious. There it is. We admitted it. We didn't feel cute enough or pretty enough or young enough or sophisticated enough or thin enough or . . . enough already! Society gives us spoken and unspoken messages and expectations regarding how we are supposed to appear. We rate our appearance when we look in the mirror or at other people. We say to ourselves, "They will (or won't) think I'm enough." In effect, we've let "them" become an audience for whom we're performing. We hear applause or boos as we interpret what we think "they" think about us. Sometimes we measure up; other times we don't. When we think we measure up, we become confident, maybe even arrogant. When we assess that we don't measure up, we become anxious or depressed. Our confidence has been taken from us. Sounds like robbery to me.

Take our appearance, for example. When does our obsession with appearance begin? Unfortunately, that journey begins early in life, as we each develop in our own culture of comparisons. Barbie had a role in that. Did you know that if Barbie were a real, life-size woman, "She would be 5′9″ tall, have a 39″ bust, an 18″ waist, 33″ hips and a size 3 shoe. . . . She likely would not menstruate . . . she'd have to walk on all fours due to her proportions."[1] Seriously? We're giving our little girls these dolls, and we're inadvertently celebrating such incomprehensible proportions. Barbie might be the first identity training tool, but she has had lots of company by the time young girls become teenagers. How do you know if you are pretty enough? You look around. How do you know if you are wearing the latest style? You look around. How do you know if your new hairstyle is going to work? You look around. How do you know if you are thin enough? You look around. You watch a movie. You see a commercial. You open a magazine. You take a trip to the mall and gaze at the models in the storefront windows. Journey to any high school, college, or even church campus, and you'll quickly pinpoint the latest set of appearance expectations. What do you see? You likely see a glaring message from a materialistic society that you just aren't enough. And let's not be fooled into thinking that pretty people are exempt from this struggle. Ask any beauty queen, and she will tell you the same. Left and right, you and I are robbed of being content in our own skins. Sadly, many industries depend on our being discontent with our appearance. We've been robbed of the satisfaction of who God created us to be—in flesh.

Skinny jeans, Wonderbras, stiletto heels, Botox, hair products, laser treatments, tanning beds, and acne cream—all products marketed to entice us to make a purchase because of our desire to improve our appearance. While one could certainly argue the effectiveness of the "skinny" jean, these products produce millions of dollars because women have a thirst for more and better when it comes to appearance. We'll pay pretty much anything to increase our self-appraised appearance.

The United States is rated number one for the amount of money spent on cosmetics. We're talking billions of dollars each year, with most women spending more on cosmetics than education in their lifetime. In both good and bad economic times, the beauty industry thrives, because it portrays physical attraction as a scarce necessity, born of an unattainable, airbrushed standard that promises power and acceptance. This is an empty promise, resulting in competition, shame, and chronic insecurities. The enemy has found a great tool for crippling our joy. It is true that a healthy sense of self is created from the inside out and attacked from the outside in.

Imagine the young college girl who works out daily to keep her body rock solid and lean. If she misses a workout, she thinks she's fat. What will happen to her self-concept, which has been dependent on her toned body, when she has a baby eight years later and struggles to shed her post-pregnancy weight? Unsurprisingly, she will feel self-conscious and inadequate as well as anxious to gain her trim body back. Those nasty emotions are the sign that this young mother has been robbed.

How about the young girl who backs out of going to the prom? She is experiencing a bad acne breakout and feels it has ruined what is supposed to be one of the best days of her life.

How about the wife who decides to get breast implants because she doesn't feel she can keep her husband's eye? She doesn't want to endure a painful surgery or a permanent alteration to her body, but she will, because she hopes it will bring her more security in her marriage.

Please understand it is not the attention to appearance that creates a problem. Rather, *it is the attachment to appearance—the idolizing of appearance*—that brings destruction and is an open door for a thief. It is important for us to distinguish between taking responsible care of the health and presentation of our bodies and fixating on appearance. The two couldn't be more distinct. It is perfectly healthy to find joy in taking care of your body and presenting yourself confidently. There is nothing sinful or destructive about exercising or wearing nice-looking clothing or fashionable accessories. Consider the wife of noble character described in Proverbs 31. We first learn that she is "virtuous" and "capable," "more precious than rubies" (v. 10 NLT), and trustworthy (see v. 11). She is an amazing woman—a mentor who is spiritually respected and emotionally strong. Interestingly, we also learn "she dresses in fine linen and purple gowns" (v. 22 NLT). This woman isn't wearing dull polyester every day, and it is perfectly okay that she doesn't. Her body is a sacred temple, just like yours and mine, and it is appropriate that she gives it warranted attention.

This noble woman has another piece of knowledge that we need to know. She recognizes that "beauty does not last" (v. 30 NLT). What a profound insight! Her security is not based on the appearance of her body or the beautiful clothing that she puts on her body. Her security is based on her fear of the Lord (see v. 30). It is *dangerous* to gain our confidence from anything that perishes, including our bodies and our appearance. Our bodies will one day decay and return to the earth (and they may already be beginning to sag their way there), so they are not worthy of our total confidence.

If at any time you experience anxiety related to your appearance, know that you have been distracted and conned by an unworthy thief. Consider Luke 12:23: "For life is more than food, and the body more than clothes." While the Scriptures were perhaps referring to the *provision* of clothing, the concept certainly applies to our discussion that the body is more than an hourglass figure.

Lest you get discouraged, let me inform you that we have stumbled on some truth that is very powerful. Remember, our eyes are the tools the thief uses in the robbery of our contentment. Wouldn't you know it—God has a word for us about this very subject. Let's gain some insight from the book of Matthew: "The eye is the lamp of the body. If your eyes are healthy, your whole body will be full of light. But if your eyes are unhealthy, your whole body will be full of darkness. If then the light within you is darkness, how great is that darkness!" (6:22–24). Our eyes are the tools of comparison, and I am praying that you and I have healthy eyes. With healthy eyes, we see and understand truth, and our entire bodies are full of light. We confront a thief who wants to blindfold our eyes; he seeks to darken our perception of ourselves. I am praying we will boldly remove the blindfold and refuse to be taken advantage of again.

VICTORY VERSE

"The eye is the lamp of the body. If your eyes are healthy, your whole body will be full of light. But if your eyes are unhealthy, your whole body will be full of darkness. If then the light within you is darkness, how great is that darkness!"

— MATTHEW 6:22–24

FREEDOM Q & A

1. What thoughts do you have when you look in a mirror? What emotions do you experience when you look in a mirror?

2. What impact does your perceived appearance have on your self-esteem?

3. Regarding your appearance, to whom do you compare yourself?

4. How is the aging process impacting your sense of security?

5. In what ways do you take care of your body? Do you consider this care to be (a) healthy, (b) obsessive, or (c) negligent? Explain your answer.

6. What lessons about female appearance did you learn as a child? How did you learn these lessons?

7. Do you ever experience negative emotions regarding your appearance? If so, what negative thoughts are associated with these emotions?

8. How do you typically act on the negative thoughts and emotions you named above regarding your appearance?

2

Success and Failure

Test anxiety and stage fright: frustrating, sometimes crippling, anxieties that are fed from a drive to perform well. We live in a performance-driven society, a cutthroat culture of individuals who strive to be the best. The top seller, the star of the show, the highest earner, the strongest man, the winner of the pageant, the head of the class. For those bent toward having anxieties, this pursuit of achievement is a perfect storm—a storm created by a need to be known. It's a need that leads to perfectionism and fear. What drives a person's obsessive focus on success? It is the avoidance of failure, perhaps even the fear of failure.

How can you know if you are overly attached to either experiences or quests of success or experiences or fears of failure? Let me ask you a few questions, and you take some time to explore your answers:

1. Are you overly discouraged or depressed if you receive a less-than-perfect score on an academic test or job-related task?

2. Does your family sometimes complain that you devote too much time to your job, school, or pursuit of your career?

Do they appreciate your achievements but sometimes get jealous of your quest for success?

3. Do you get overly angry when others interfere with your attempts to succeed or when someone else's incompetence impacts your success?

4. Do you feel you ride an emotional roller coaster that is based on your perception of success or failure in various aspects of your life?

5. Do you withdraw from activities or challenges due to the fear that you might fail?

6. Do you minimize risks, only following through with challenges you are absolutely certain you will successfully master?

7. Do you have low expectations for yourself? Do you sometimes think, *If I expect to fail, then it won't hurt as bad when I actually do fail?*

8. Do you privately see yourself as having more value than others because of your drive and ability to succeed?

9. Do you feel your previous failures have defined you as a person?

10. Do you feel your worth is connected to your achievements in life?

If you answered yes to any of these questions, then you likely have been the victim of identity theft. It's almost impossible to avoid falling victim to some degree. You see, as we discussed earlier, we have an enemy, and he desires to steal our joy and contentment. Overachievers and underachievers are in the same boat. They've both been deceived by a convincing accuser, and their emotions and actions reflect the lies they believe.

When did this drive for success begin? Let's look back and see if any of these ring a bell: end-of-grade tests, VIP, academically gifted, follower, benchwarmer, GPA, IQ, loser. If you're caught up in this form of identity theft, the seeds were likely planted in your elementary years and watered by friends and family, teachers and coaches. These people wanted to see you reach your full potential and never intended to bring you harm. The enemy can manipulate well-intentioned situations and people to bring about his plans for deception.

Consider the young girl who has always made straight As. She is embarrassed when she is named for the A/B honor roll because she is one point away from an A in science, making this her first B ever. She wonders what everyone will think of her and feels she has disappointed her parents and teachers, despite their efforts to challenge that false belief. A thief wants her joy and contentment.

Consider the woman who has traditionally excelled in her job. She is a go-getter, a leader, and is known for her dependability and success at work. She has always received accolades from her supervisors and has never received a negative comment on a performance evaluation. This success has driven her and given her great confidence in herself. Much to her surprise, when a new supervisor is hired, his feedback is different. In fact, he is critical of her performance. She is crushed and flooded with thoughts of inadequacy. She is so nervous about his feedback that she can hardly focus. She is terrified of failure and now feels she is on the brink of her worst fear coming true.

How about the young woman who decides not to apply to graduate school for physical therapy? She doesn't want to face the possibility of rejection. She feels God has been leading her to become a physical therapist, and she is a talented, bright young woman. But she denies her dream to ensure she doesn't have to face the pain of failure. Playing it safe seems like a more realistic alternative. She doesn't have to worry about disappointment if her expectations are lowered.

Like appearance, success and failure in and of themselves are not problems. We will succeed in some areas of our lives and fail in others. These experiences are normal. It is not success or failure that jeopardizes our self-worth. It is our *attachment* to experiences/quests for success or experiences/fears of failure that brings destruction and opens the door for the thief. Success can inadvertently become an idol that traps us and lies to us about who we really are. Although we know some of the most successful people in the world are those who have learned from their failures, we may experience such a fear of failure that we avoid any opportunity to benefit from its many lessons. When we give success or failure too much power in our lives, we are set up for struggle. Friend, if you experience excessive amounts of positive or negative emotion related to success or failure, then you've been distracted and conned by an unworthy thief.

If our current measures of success are stumbling blocks to a healthy identity, what is our measure supposed to be? What if I said success is defined by whether you accomplish your purpose in this life? Lest that thought overwhelm or confuse you, let me just share that in Scripture, God clearly defines success as seeking Him and allowing His power to be made perfect in us. Consider Paul's words to the church in Corinth:

> But he said to me, "My grace is sufficient for you, for my power is made perfect in weakness." Therefore I will boast all the more gladly about my weaknesses, so that Christ's power may rest on me. That is why, for Christ's sake, I delight in weaknesses, in insults, in hardships, in persecutions, in difficulties. For when I am weak, then I am strong. (2 Cor. 12:9–10)

God is much less interested in our successes or failures, in our various tasks or assignments, than He is in our pursuit of a relationship with Him and our willingness to allow Him to perfect our weaknesses. That is success this side of eternity, my friend. If we will pursue Him, then He will give back to us something that success never could: joy and contentment.

King Solomon, a man remembered for his success and wisdom, recorded his experience on the subject of how we view success:

I wanted to see what was good for people to do under the heavens during the few days of their lives; I undertook great projects: I built houses for myself and planted vineyards. I made gardens and parks and planted all kinds of fruit trees in them. . . . I became greater by far than anyone in Jerusalem before me. In all this my wisdom stayed with me.

> I denied myself nothing my eyes desired;
>   I refused my heart no pleasure.
> My heart took delight in all my labor,
>   and this was the reward for all my toil.
> Yet when I surveyed all that my hands had done
>   and what I had toiled to achieve,
> everything was meaningless, a chasing after the wind;
>   nothing was gained under the sun. . . .

I hated all the things I had toiled for under the sun, because I must leave them to the one who comes after me. . . . So my heart began to despair over all my toilsome labor under the sun. For a person may labor with wisdom, knowledge and skill, and then they must leave all they own to another who has not toiled for it. This too is meaningless and a great misfortune. What do people get for all the toil and anxious striving with which they labor under the sun? All their days their work is grief and pain; even at night their minds do not rest. This too is meaningless.

A person can do nothing better than to eat and drink and find satisfaction in their own toil. This too, I see, is from the hand of God, for without him, who can eat or find enjoyment? To the person who pleases him, God gives wisdom, knowledge and happiness, but to the sinner he gives the task of gathering and storing up wealth to hand it over to the one who pleases God. This too is meaningless, a chasing after the wind. (Eccles. 2:3–5, 9–11, 18, 20–26)

Solomon later recognized that "all toil and all achievement spring from one person's envy of another," and he identified this as "meaningless" (Eccles. 4:4). King Solomon noticed in humankind a tendency to compare and want to "keep up with the Joneses," a meaningless but enduring pursuit, ignited by an enemy whose sole goal is to distract and ultimately prevent us from pursuing a loving God.

So, you see, the tendency to get caught up in our worldly success or failure has been a temptation since the origin of humanity. But, let's take the advice of wise King Solomon; let's see our striving for achievement or our resistance to try for what they really are: *meaningless* this side of heaven. I challenge you to refocus your efforts for success on seeking the One who created you, for one day He desires to look at you and say: "Well done, my good and faithful servant" (Matt. 25:21 NLT). That is true success.

VICTORY VERSE

"To the person who pleases him, God gives wisdom, knowledge and happiness, but to the sinner he gives the task of gathering and storing up wealth to hand it over to the one who pleases God. This too is meaningless, a chasing after the wind."

ECCLESIASTES 2:26

FREEDOM Q & A

1. Step back in your mind and look at your life. Are you "chasing after the wind"? Solomon described a man who was lonely, who poured himself into his success but still couldn't find contentment (see Eccles. 4:8). Would this describe you? Why or why not?

2. How have you overly identified yourself with your successes? How have you overly identified yourself with your failures?

3. What emotions do you experience in regard to your successes/failures? Do you ride a roller coaster of emotions?

4. Read Colossians 3:23–24. God speaks often through His Word about the value of work and His desire that we work in a way that honors Him. How does this instruction fit with your current concept of success and failure and where your rewards will originate?

3

Approval and Rejection

D o you remember those notes that kids passed around the halls of your elementary school? "Do you like me? Check 'yes,' 'no,' 'maybe.'" Some kids can't resist finding out if that someone special feels the same about them. I'll never forget a few years ago when one of my sons revealed to me that he had a crush on a little girl, and he suspected she felt the same way about him. Then he disclosed that he had not talked to her in over a year. "Why?" I asked, surprised. "Because I might say the wrong thing and then she won't like me. Then I'd be really, really sad." What a profoundly fitting statement in light of this chapter.

We are wired for relationships. Our fellowship with others is crucial to our emotional and spiritual health, and our need for healthy connections starts at infancy. A baby who cries out and receives the caring response of a parent develops a healthy attachment. This bond sets the stage for the child's ability to connect with others later in life. But infants whose needs are ignored, whose cries are routinely rejected, don't develop these bonds and are vulnerable to attachment disorders later in development. The approval or rejection of others is powerful.

To further make the point, consider how isolation is used in the prison system. Solitary confinement has been a widely used form of punishment for decades. It is also considered a form of psychological torture, causing irreparable psychological damage and mental illness. Why such serious effects? Because without the interaction, acceptance, and involvement of other human beings, we don't function well.

Perhaps the fact that we don't function well outside of relationships with others is what makes the subject of this chapter so tricky. You see, there's nothing wrong with receiving the approval of people you care about. In fact, it's hoped and expected that you will have at least some form of approval from them. It's also expected that some people will reject us, as it is impossible to make, and keep, everyone happy. Approval and rejection in and of themselves are not the problem. The problem lies when approval and rejection are given *control* in our lives. Being *overly attached* to the approval or rejection of others brings destruction and opens the door for a thief.

Many of the clients I see in my office are driven by a need for approval and an avoidance of rejection. Some might get their security from being part of what would be considered the "popular" crowd—they feel secure because these particular people approve of them. They work desperately to maintain that approval. Others may struggle with insecurities resulting from painful experiences of rejection. They connect their personal worth to those experiences. As a result, they may feel unloved or unworthy. In both cases, these people have given power and control to the traps of approval or rejection, which influence how they see themselves, their decisions, their relationships, and, ultimately, their joy. When this happens, it's easy to see that seeking approval or avoiding rejection prevents us from having a stable and secure identity. To determine if this vulnerability regarding approval and rejection applies to you, let's consider a few questions:

1. Have you dated someone you really didn't think was "the one" because you were afraid to be alone?
2. Is it difficult for you to say no to others?
3. Do you feel unusually elated when people admire or notice you?
4. Are you crushed to the point of feeling depressed when someone you admire ignores you?
5. Is it difficult for you to hear criticism?
6. Do you avoid close relationships to prevent opening yourself up to the risk of rejection?
7. Do you sometimes find yourself trying to impress others?
8. Do you tolerate inappropriate behavior in others because you find it too difficult to set boundaries?
9. Do you work tirelessly to try to gain the approval of particular people in your life?
10. Do you avoid confrontations with others for fear of the impact they will have on your relationships?

If you answered yes to any of these questions, then welcome to the majority. Many of us have been deceived into feeling we *must* have the approval of a particular person: a parent, a spouse, a pastor or church leader, an employer, a friend, etc. For those who unintentionally make the quest for approval an idol, the cost becomes significant—sometimes financially, but always emotionally and spiritually. This quest may rule your life and monopolize your time. It may even cause you to make unwise decisions. If this describes you, please know that you have been deceived. Undoubtedly, you ride an emotional roller coaster based on whether your quest for approval is successful. This distracts you from securing true joy and contentment. Sounds like another threat to your identity, doesn't it?

Consider the teenager whose father abandoned her at a young age. Now that she's at a time in her life when males are giving her the attention she so craves, she loses her virginity to a teenage boy who convinces her that if she makes this compromise, she will win his love. Her thirst for approval costs her a price she never intended to pay.

How about the woman in her forties who divorced when she was thirty? When she learned of her husband's affair, she experienced his rejection so painfully that she could hardly function. She has since felt that he cheated on her because she was unworthy of his love. Now, a decade later, she doesn't allow others to get too close to her, and she has few friends. She will not even consider dating again. She is so fearful of another painful rejection that she chooses instead to live in isolation. It is a "safe" but miserably lonely existence.

And then there is the retired woman who, after working so much during her grandchildren's lives, is so excited to have time away from her job to spend time getting to know her grandchildren. But having been disconnected from their grandmother for so long, the grandchildren won't have much to do with her. She battles with feelings of rejection and is constantly on a quest for their approval. She buys them item after item in an attempt to gain their attention and love. They seem to respond for a little while but then ignore her again—until the next purchase. She's going into credit card debt in an effort to secure their love and, ultimately, feel whole. Her need for their approval is costing her financially and emotionally.

If you've made it through grade school, then you've already tasted the pangs of rejection. The world can be cruel. If you've been rejected by those you should have been able to count on, then I suspect the thief uses this rejection against you. If you believe, because of past rejections, that you are unlovable, inadequate, or unworthy, then you have been deceived. You may sometimes think something is wrong with you that caused that person to abandon you. The truth is, every human being in your life will disappoint you on some level, but this has no bearing on your innate value. Let me also remind you that God makes some promises about the issue of rejection: "Never will I leave you; never will I forsake you" (Heb. 13:5). He is the only One who can make and follow through with that promise. Unfortunately, you may find it difficult to trust His steadfastness as a result of painful rejections at the hands of others in your past.

Surely this topic of approval and rejection is a tender one for our Lord. You see, Scripture tells us that Jesus was "despised and rejected by men. . . . He was despised, and we esteemed Him not" (Isa. 53:3 ESV). Jesus knows what it is like to be rejected. To have others disapprove of Him. Remember, Jesus was, and continues to be, rejected by those He gave His life to save.

God loves you so much that it creates in Him a jealousy for you (now there's the flip side to rejection if I've ever seen it). He desires to compete with no one. If you realize your quest for approval is an idol, please confess that to God now. Ask Him to heal that perceived need in you, allowing you to be truly satisfied by the approval of your Creator. This confession and decision to walk away from the idolatry will free you to pursue Him, with the assurance that there is no approval to be earned and rejection isn't a possibility. You will never find a safer relationship in life.

In case you aren't aware of just how safe this relationship is, let me share with you how your Creator feels about you. For those who acknowledge Jesus as Savior and Lord, He refers to you as His "handiwork" (Eph. 2:10). He says you are adopted, "chosen," and "included in Christ" (Eph. 1:5, 11, 13). Look to Zephaniah 3:17 for a refreshing image of God's tenderness toward you, as His child: "The LORD your God is with you, the Mighty Warrior who saves. He will take great delight in you; in his love he will no longer rebuke you, but will rejoice over you with singing." What an incredible image. He rejoices over you in song. As we come to the end of this chapter, I encourage you to rejoice in your Father's approval of you. His love for you that will never cease!

VICTORY VERSE

"The LORD your God is with you, the Mighty Warrior who saves. He will take great delight in you; in his love he will no longer rebuke you, but will rejoice over you with singing."

ZEPHANIAH 3:17

FREEDOM Q & A

1. Consider your answers to the series of questions in this chapter that assess the control approval and/or rejection have in your life. Describe your reaction to your answers.

2. From which particular people in your life do you feel you need approval?

   What is your *emotional reaction* when you *receive* this approval? (How do you feel?)

   What is your *behavioral reaction* when you *receive* this approval? (How do you act?)

   What is your *emotional reaction* when you *do not receive* this approval? (How do you feel?)

   What is your *behavioral reaction* when you *do not receive* this approval? (How do you act?)

3. Describe an experience of rejection from your past that has had a profound impact on your sense of self. What is God speaking to you about this past experience and the impact it has had?

4. God speaks often through His Word about His tender love for you as well as His promise never to abandon you. What is your reaction to these words?

5. Reread the victory verse from this chapter. What thoughts do you have about this Scripture? Are you able to accept that God "rejoice[s] over you with singing"? Why or why not?

4

Life Experiences
and Trauma

My life will never be the same again." Some experiences are defining experiences. They shape us in ways we never desired. Perhaps never intended. Many of these experiences are unplanned and unwelcomed. We didn't see them coming. All kinds of experiences can potentially shape our identity, if given the power to do so. Unfortunately, the unthinkable encounters are often the ones with the most influence. We don't realize they are defining us. All the while, they are subtly, but powerfully, changing how we think. How we respond to situations. How we see ourselves. Trauma is a powerful thief.

If you've had some challenging life experiences, you're going to be tempted to skip over this chapter. You don't want to be reminded. I understand. No one wants to gaze on pain. But if you want freedom from your insecurity, you need to gaze, even if only for a short time, in order to determine the degree to which those experiences have hindered your wholeness.

So, take a deep breath, and be honest with yourself. Why? Because you really want to be whole.

1. Have you ever witnessed or experienced a situation that was difficult for you to process (perhaps it caused flashbacks or nightmares)?
2. Do you suffer from any difficult diagnoses (physical or psychological)?
3. Have you experienced challenges that seem unfair?
4. Have you ever been treated neglectfully, abusively, or violently by another person?
5. Have you directly encountered a tragedy in life?
6. Have you been touched inappropriately at any point in your life?
7. Do you sometimes feel that your past will prevent you from having a good future?
8. Were you the target of bullying in childhood (in a school or home environment)?
9. Do you struggle with regret? Choices you have made? Choices others have made for you?
10. Have you previously treated others in a way that it is now difficult for you to accept?

Take another deep breath. If you're like most people, you just encountered a very uncomfortable moment. But this is important. Otherwise I wouldn't suggest any reason to invite discomfort.

Now ponder with me. If you answered yes to any of these questions, how do you think those life experiences have robbed you? How have they influenced how you see yourself? Were certain thoughts about yourself introduced with these events? Did shame present itself in your life? Have you felt damaged? Hopeless? Unworthy of looking forward to your future? Have you felt stuck since those experiences? How has your life been changed as a result of those experiences? Consider the power of those experiences in negatively shaping your identity.

Let's consider the woman who was raped at a college party after an unknown offender slipped a drug into her drink. For years following the assault, she felt that the incident had changed her. She was a virgin previous to the rape and couldn't get past the feeling that she was now "dirty." She's wrestled with shame and false guilt regarding what happened, exacerbated by the unsupportive responses of seemingly safe mentors, which ultimately left her with feelings of worthlessness. "Since I am going to be treated as if I don't have worth anyway, there's no need in having any more boundaries"—this was the reasoning that began to facilitate the promiscuity that further left her feeling shame. This traumatic life experience altered her sense of who she was, her value. Years later, she still struggles to separate the incident from herself.

How about the young woman who was in a car accident that caused her to be paralyzed from the waist down. Her day-to-day activities are now radically altered as she adjusts to a new normal. Psychologically, she struggles with accepting the change and its limitations. She wrestles with thoughts that she is "less than a woman" and "defective." Separating her identity from her limitations seems nearly impossible, which has taken a toll on her self-worth, causing her to become depressed and withdrawn.

Consider the woman who spent her teenage years bullying most of the girls in her class. She called them names, started rumors about them, sought to embarrass them in front of others, picked fights, and basically just enjoyed making their lives miserable. Now, as an adult, she feels horrible about how she treated her female classmates. She feels she can never show her face at a high school reunion. She feels undeserving of forgiveness and that her previous reputation will prevent her from enjoying life in her community for the rest of her life.

Contemplate this Scripture with me:

Who will bring any charge against those whom God has chosen? It is God who justifies. Who then is the one who condemns? No one. Christ Jesus who died—more than that, who was raised to life—is at the right hand of God and is also interceding for us. Who shall separate us from the love of Christ? Shall trouble or hardship or persecution or famine or nakedness or danger or sword? . . . No, in all these things we are more than conquerors through him who loved us. For I am convinced that neither death nor life, neither angels nor demons, neither the present nor the future, nor any powers, neither height nor depth, nor anything else in all creation, will be able to separate us from the love of God that is in Christ Jesus our Lord. (Rom. 8:33–35, 37–39)

I don't know your story or your history. Perhaps you grew up in the home of an alcoholic. Maybe you were sexually abused as a child or bullied as a teen. You may have regrets about previous choices that severed relationships, blocked aspirations, or caused you great grief. Listen, my friends, challenging life events *can* condemn us, but *only* if we allow them to do so. Even so, these experiences can never separate us from God's love. Unfortunately, suffering is a normal part of the human condition. We all face tough circumstances, effects of past regrets, seemingly unfair obstacles, and sometimes even unthinkable tragedies. Everyone has a story. The problem occurs when these challenges are given the space to *define* us. As we've seen in previous chapters, a life experience or traumatic event is not the problem; it is the uninvited and unintended *attachment* to that experience that brings destruction and opens the door for the thief. Sister, *life experiences cannot be allowed to bring a charge against you*! Let God, not experiences, do the defining, separating earthly struggles and traumas from your inherent worth. This separation of the *event* from your *identity* is crucial!

Go back and review that Scripture from Romans 8 once more. If you struggle with the consequences of a challenging life experience, you have likely developed some skills for coping, some methods for surviving what you have endured. There's nothing wrong with coping skills; in fact, they are necessary in the face of tough obstacles. But if you are struggling with your worth, you have also likely developed some *destructive* coping skills—skills that may be directly preventing you from becoming whole and may even be inviting additional, unnecessary suffering or shame. Examples of destructive coping skills include withdrawal, promiscuity, substance use, and eating disorders. Using a destructive coping skill that only invites more struggle and suffering makes a traumatic event doubly tragic. You read the Scriptures that call you a conqueror in the face of hardship, danger, threat . . . and you feel anything but a conqueror. But can you imagine? Just imagine the freedom to embrace being *"more* than a conqueror." This freedom is at your fingertips when you allow God, rather than your experience, to define you. That freedom is yours when you shed any poor coping skills, any inaccurate attachment to life events, and any false beliefs regarding your identity.

For years, secular researchers have validated the effect of trauma in negatively impacting a person's self-esteem. Now they're also confirming the influence of religiosity on diminishing that impact.[1] What does that mean for you and me? It means that when we invite God into our lives and into our pain, *His healing stabilizes the negative effects of trauma.* In other words, His defining of us is more powerful than the negative impact of our life experiences. God constructs your resilience—not only in your daily functioning but also in your self-worth.

If you want to be whole, gaze on tough circumstances just long enough to accept God's redefining (His opinion about how this experience defines you) and agree with His perspective on your worth. God doesn't see you as a culmination of your life experiences. When He looks at you, He doesn't see that traumatic event. If you have trusted Him as Savior and Lord, then when He looks at you, He sees His child. Holy and blameless. His masterpiece. He has no difficulty separating your sin from your value. And

He has no difficulty separating your traumas, challenges, and life experiences from your value. Those tough life experiences you are thinking about right now—they do not define you in God's eyes. Therefore, they no longer have to define you in your own eyes. You don't have to be stuck because of life's hurts anymore. Remember, God's healing stabilizes the negative effects of trauma. Let Him heal you. Let His perspective overpower your own perspective. Agree with Him. Give Him the burden of that traumatic heartache, for His yoke is easy and His burden is light (see Matt. 11:30). He will give you rest from the journey of carrying something burdensome far too long. This is the day to begin bouncing back and accepting your innate worth, which your hurts can never alter. (For more discussion about developing resilience, I invite you to read my book *Becoming Resilient: How to Move through Suffering and Come Back Stronger.*)

Perhaps you are one of a handful of people reading this chapter who has been sheltered and buffered from some of the challenging struggles you have seen others experience. Maybe you have had the privilege of encountering certain positive experiences in life that others have only dreamed about. If anything, life experiences have caused you to feel great about yourself. Let's thank God for the protection you've experienced and some of the special opportunities you've been privileged to have. But please be careful, my friend. Judging your worth by anything temporal will eventually prove to be a stumbling block in your wholeness. One day you will encounter trials and struggles. Maybe even tragedy. If your security is based on the wonderful experiences you've encountered in life, you will be set up to be immobilized by the inevitable struggles you will face. Remember, resist giving these life experiences the power to define you. So, enjoy the peace and protection you have experienced, but don't let them define you any more than you would expect a tragedy should be given space to define another sister in Christ. Those who meet life's inevitable tragedies with resilience have a healthy foundation prior to those traumatic experiences. Make sure your foundation is whole and can serve as a source of stability for any future storm you may encounter.°

VICTORY VERSE

"Who shall separate us from the love of Christ? Shall trouble or hardship or persecution or famine or nakedness or danger or sword? . . . No, in all these things we are more than conquerors through him who loved us."

— ROMANS 8:35, 37

FREEDOM Q & A

1. Consider your answers to the questions on the checklist. If you answered yes to any of those questions, how do you think those experiences have influenced how you see yourself? What negative thoughts were introduced following those events?

2. How have those events and corresponding thoughts impacted your emotions? How have they impacted your behaviors and choices?

3. How have you coped with the consequences of these experiences? Have you had any destructive coping skills that have invited additional, unnecessary suffering?

°If this chapter has been exceptionally tough for you to read, then perhaps you have unresolved wounds resulting from painful past experiences. You can bounce back. But you may need some help. Reach out today, before you change your mind. Contact a trusted mentor, pastor, or professional Christian counselor. You don't have to walk this journey alone.

4. We've established that life experiences can't be allowed to bring a charge against you. Can you imagine separating these experiences from your inherent worth? If so, think about the following:

What impact might that separation have on your thoughts about yourself?

What impact might it have on your emotional stability?

What impact might it have on your future choices?

5. Take the time to pray about any life experiences that have brought a charge against you. What do you sense God wants to reveal to you regarding how painful experiences have negatively impacted your self-worth?

5

Roles and Responsibilities

I remember the brokenness I saw in the eyes of a middle-aged woman sitting across from me. Her youngest child had just moved out of the home, fulfilling her dream to attend college. My client had enjoyed the role of being a mother for decades. She had poured herself completely into the lives of her children. That was no small task, as her "quiver" had been full with children spread across nearly two decades. But now her home was empty. And so was she. She still enjoyed connections with her children from a distance, but it wasn't the same. She had succeeded in raising her children to be independent and purposeful. But now she was the one feeling dependent and without purpose. The house was quiet. And she was lost. How would she spend her time? How could God use her now? Was there anyone who needed her? Did she have anything to offer? How could she bear the silence in her home that was nearly deafening to the ear? She wept, feeling useless and without worth outside of her responsibility as a mother. She grieved as if there had been a death. I suppose in a sense there had been—the death of her daily responsibilities.

The empty nest is one of life's many transitions that has the potential to expose a person's unhealthy attachment to a life role or responsibility. When we unconsciously place too much value on a temporary task or duty, and then our circumstances change, we can experience an identity crisis. This is a challenging place to be; a time filled with intense negative emotions and a sense of anxiety, chaos, and uneasiness. This is what happened to my client. Unintentionally, she had poured everything about herself into her role as a mother. So much so that when those responsibilities were complete and it was time for a healthy transition, there was nothing else left of her. She had attached her worth to her role without ever realizing it. But when her children left the home, she had to face the rude awakening of her brokenness. She had to sort out who she was apart from the needs of her children.

Can you relate? Consider the questions below as potentially indicative of a similar struggle you may face regarding your roles and responsibilities:

1. When someone asks you to describe yourself, do you usually respond by listing your roles or responsibilities (wife, mother, stay-at-home mom, occupation, etc.)?

2. When you experience a transition or loss of a role or responsibility, do you feel excessively painful negative emotions?

3. Do you ever feel you are living vicariously through your children or that you are overly attached to their activities or successes? Would others consider you a "trophy parent"?

4. Did you find retirement, or the empty nest, has brought about a period of emotional instability? (Or do you expect it might if you haven't encountered it yet?)

5. Do you sometimes feel as though you are losing yourself through your caregiving of other people?

6. Are you often exhausted as a result of being spread too thin with responsibilities?

7. Do you find yourself volunteering to participate in or lead numerous activities, committees, organizations, or projects?

8. Do you sometimes feel inadequate because your various roles in life aren't as you once had expected (unplanned childlessness, job loss, singlehood, etc.)?

9. Do others consider you a "workaholic"? Do you feel that you are overly dedicated to your career?

10. Do you sense that a large part of your self-worth (positively or negatively) is attached to your life roles or responsibilities?

We all have roles in life. Roles define what we do with our time and how we use our strengths and abilities. These responsibilities are important. We may be a child, a parent, a spouse, a friend, an employee, a member of a church, an athlete on a team, or a student. God has plans for our lives, and therefore has appointed various roles to each of us. Nothing is innately wrong with roles or responsibilities in life. But when we are *overly attached* to those roles, when our identity is overly connected to our responsibilities, then we are positioned for an emotional roller coaster. Maybe even an identity crisis. We've all heard the phrase "The only constant in life is change." How true! This applies to our roles and responsibilities in life as well. They will change. We will experience positive adjustments, such as a new baby, a wedding, a promotion, and a new friendship. We may also experience painful changes, such as a divorce, a layoff, infertility, the death of a family member, a geographical move that distances us from our friends and church family, or an injury. If we are overly attached to a role or responsibility prior to a transition, then we enter into the makings of a perfect storm—the onslaught of an identity crisis.

Consider the young woman who prided herself in and identified herself according to her role as a track athlete. She received a full scholarship to run in college. Then an accident caused a permanent injury, resulting in a change in her competitive ability.

Now her struggle isn't limited to the physical pain she experiences or the expected grief of the loss of her collegiate running opportunities. Her struggle is further complicated by an identity crisis. *If I can't run competitively, then who am I?* she wonders. She wrestles with self-loathing because she is no longer who she once saw herself as being.

Let's also consider the woman who has dreamed of being a wife and mother since she was a small child. She's held on to these goals in an effort to feel "complete," having always felt empty, that something was missing. When life didn't turn out the way she'd always expected, she began to feel even more empty, worthless, and depressed. At the age of forty, she never thought she'd be single and without children. She has built her identity on the expectation of being a wife and mother, and now she feels more incomplete than ever.

And then there's the woman who's known to her family as a "workaholic." She has excelled in her job and is an extremely capable and competent person. She finds it difficult to say no when her help is requested, so she often spreads herself too thin. She feels an emotional high when she is affirmed for her work, and she is crushed when someone higher up expresses disappointment in her job performance. Her sense of self-worth is closely aligned with her job, and retirement is quickly approaching. She can't imagine how she'll feel about herself when she no longer has the responsibility of this job.

Remember, our roles or responsibilities in life are not the problem. Our inadvertent idolizing of those roles and attachment to those responsibilities bring destruction and open the door for a thief. This distinction is vitally important. If you feel anxiety about maintaining your roles or potentially transitioning from your responsibilities, then you have been distracted and conned by an unworthy thief.

Our roles in life are strictly vessels for accomplishing God's will. We go outside His will when we allow those roles to define us, regardless of whether the defining is favorable or unfavorable. The danger? Roles will inevitably change. If we're attached to those roles, we'll feel empty and purposeless in their absence, like the individuals we've discussed. Responsibilities in life *will* adjust with time and circumstance, but our identity is to be unchanging and stable. Immovable.

Want to hear about a role and responsibility we can fully embrace? It is our place in the body of Christ. We each have a role in that body. "For just as each of us has one body with many members, and these members do not all have the same function, so in Christ we, though many, form one body, and each member belongs to all the others" (Rom. 12:4–5). My role is naturally different from yours, and yours from mine. But, as His children, we are all members of His body.

Though our roles may differ, our measure of value and responsibility to the body is the same. Read these instructive words from 1 Corinthians: "Those parts of the body that seem to be weaker are indispensable, and the parts that we think are less honorable we treat with special honor" (12:22–23). God designs and assigns our roles and responsibilities, and sees each part as "indispensable." So, what view are we to have regarding our role in the body of Christ? We are not to think too lowly of ourselves—or too highly of ourselves. We are to maintain a sober judgment, a healthy humility and assessment of who we are and our purpose within His body (see Rom. 12:3). We are not to think too little or too much of ourselves. We are simply to agree with God's estimation.

Let's be on guard. Our roles and responsibilities, when in transition, can be a tool the enemy uses to create crisis. To condemn. To shame. God sees the value of our roles differently than we do. And, during a transition, rather than pouring out condemnation, He pours out compassion and restoration. If you are struggling with a transition and realize your attachment to a role or responsibility has unintentionally invited undue suffering, then be comforted by the words of this verse: "Do not be afraid; you will not be put to shame. Do not fear disgrace; you will not be humiliated. You will forget the shame of your youth and remember no more the reproach of your widowhood" (Isa. 54:4). It is fine for us to embrace a task that God has called us to, but we must ensure that our *attachment* goes only to Him. Our identity must be in *being with Him*, rather than *doing for Him*. That is a freedom that no transition can take away. A freedom that prevents an identity crisis.

VICTORY VERSE

"For just as each of us has one body with many members, and these members do not all have the same function, so in Christ we, though many, form one body, and each member belongs to all the others."

— ROMANS 12:4–5

FREEDOM Q & A

1. Answer this question: Who am I? What do you notice about how you answered this question? Is your answer heavily associated with your roles and responsibilities in life? If so, what is your attachment to those tasks? How do your attachments to those tasks impact your self-worth?

2. Finding balance is tricky. How are you balancing embracing God's purposes for you with guarding against being overly attached to your various roles and responsibilities?

3. Consider transitions you have experienced. Were any of them complicated by your attachment to a role or responsibility? If so, how did you ultimately maneuver that transition and what did you learn from it?

4. Consider inevitable future transitions you will experience. How are you feeling about approaching those changes? What are you learning that may prepare you to embrace those transitions more smoothly?

5. How do you view your role in the body of Christ? What do you consider to be your value in the tasks God has called you to perform? Do you have a healthy, sober judgment?

6

Background and Origin

I sat across from a beautiful young woman. She had strikingly attractive features, with a nearly perfect complexion and one of the most gorgeous skin tones I had ever seen. My client was mixed race—her mother was African American and her father was Caucasian. She spoke painfully of the experiences of her origin: "I never fit in with anyone. My skin was either too light or too dark. And our family was rarely accepted. People judged my parents because they weren't the same race, and they rejected me because I was a mix of the two." The reactions of the children of her youth tainted her own view and acceptance of herself. She was unable to see beyond her own skin color. She couldn't accept the truth regarding how physically beautiful she was. She was also unable to see her value apart from the feedback she had received, regarding something as insignificant as the pigment of her skin.

Our identity can be hijacked by anything. Even things totally out of our control, like innate personal characteristics or circumstantial factors in our childhood. We're going to discuss some of these highly significant influencers of our self-worth in this chapter. Let's begin identifying vulnerabilities by answering the questions in the checklist below. As you answer, remember that you are answering based on your perception of yourself, rather than perceptions or stereotypes others may have of you.

1. Do you feel that your sense of self is strongly influenced (positively or negatively) by your childhood socioeconomic status?

2. Have innate, involuntary characteristics (such as race, skin color, hair color, stature, body type, or gender) impacted your perception of your personal value?

3. Have you felt that others were superior or inferior to you because they were raised with different resources or opportunities?

4. Has an adoption or childhood history of foster care/orphanage placement impacted the development of your personal identity (favorably or unfavorably)?

5. Have the dynamics of growing up in a single-parent home or a blended family impacted your view of yourself?

6. Has your belief in yourself been influenced by growing up in the home of an overly authoritarian or overly permissive parent?

7. Has your birth order or being an only child affected your sense of self?

8. Did growing up in a healthy and supportive church or a church with false teachings sway your self-image?

9. Do you feel the development of your personal identity was shaped by your being the child of a pastor or prominent person in the community, causing you to experience a "glasshouse" childhood?

10. Did growing up as a "third-culture kid"—perhaps as the child of an international missionary or a military parent—impact your perception of yourself?

11. Do you presently struggle with your age, feeling you are too young or too old for significant purpose?

God designed our self-worth to be as constant and unmovable as our gender or the color of our skin. Unfortunately, we live in a world that makes that stability challenging and even uses inherent qualities against us. If you struggle with some of the topics in the checklist above, you have likely felt helpless to address your self-worth. Why? Because nothing in your developmental history was within your control. We cannot control genetics. Nor, as children, can we direct the conditions of our culture or environment or the decisions of our parents. Though our self-worth is not automatically and completely formed by these factors, they certainly can be influences. For some, they are significant influences. Sometimes the enemy uses these factors to radically steal a stable identity. We must address this theft if we are going to be rescued from a destructive belief regarding our value.

For example, a teenage girl has a tremendous passion for teaching others about Christ, but she cowers down and hides behind others. Why does she behave this way? Because she feels inadequate. She is female, and she is young. She's been told that women have no role in teaching the gospel, and that there is no place for young people in ministry. She takes the feedback and applies it too closely to her soul. These innate characteristics have circumvented her value and she feels of little worth as a result. She questions her purpose and calling.

Consider the woman who was adopted as an infant. Despite the nurturing love shown to her by her adoptive parents and their consistent attempts to assure her that her biological mother made a loving but painful choice in giving her up for adoption, she has always struggled with feeling abandoned, unworthy, inadequate, and rejected. This cruel attack on her self-worth has led to years of pain.

And what about the woman who grew up in poverty and also grew into the belief that a person's value is related to their financial status. Even as an adult, she feels she doesn't measure up because she doesn't have the level of wealth she sees others enjoy. She exhausts herself with comparisons, always striving to keep up with her financial goals to feel satisfied with herself as a person.

As with the other identity thieves, our innate characteristics or the conditions of our origin are not problems. Our *attachment* to these things brings destruction and opens the door for a thief. If you experience negative emotions related to your background, origin, or innate characteristics, then you have likely been distracted and conned by an unworthy thief who wants to convince you that these uncontrollable conditions are a reflection of your worth.

Let's consider a biblical example. Moses was born at a time when being born a Hebrew boy was the equivalent of a death sentence. To save his life, his mother delicately placed him into a basket and allowed him to float down the Nile River, where she anticipated he would be saved from danger. She was correct, and little Moses was rescued by Pharaoh's daughter and adopted into Pharaoh's family. This wasn't just any family. This was the most powerful family in Egypt. Moses grew up as a prince and had access to anything he could have wanted. But Moses never emotionally disconnected from his Hebrew roots. In fact, when he was a young man, he murdered an Egyptian after witnessing him beating a Hebrew slave. Moses fled Egypt but soon discovered he wasn't welcomed by the Hebrews either. He was rejected by his Egyptian *and* Hebrew roots. Moses became a refugee, with no place to call home. He was a third-culture kid in an identity crisis.

Did Moses overcome his identity crisis? He absolutely did. And it's a good thing he did, because he would play a vital role in Israel's liberation. According to Hebrews 11:

> By faith Moses, when he had grown up, refused to be known as the son of Pharaoh's daughter. He chose to be mistreated along with the people of God rather than to enjoy the fleeting pleasures of sin. He regarded disgrace for the sake of Christ as of greater value than the treasures of Egypt, because he was looking ahead to his reward. By faith he left Egypt, not fearing the king's anger; he persevered because he saw him who is invisible. By faith he kept

the Passover and the application of blood, so that the destroyer of the firstborn would not touch the firstborn of Israel. (vv. 24–28)

Moses ultimately rejected his Egyptian heritage and embraced his purpose in leading God's people. Had he been distracted by the benefits of his upbringing, he would have missed his purpose, which he came to understand as being of "greater value."

"Before I formed you in the womb I knew you" (Jer. 1:5). These words remind us that God had His eyes on us and His hands were leading us before we were even conceived. Indeed, we are "fearfully and wonderfully made" because our Creator is our true foundation (Ps. 139:13–14). *He is our background and origin!* God's presence in our formation and His design of our purpose are far more significant than the impact of any part of our heritage, our culture, or our innate physical characteristics. And, as if those facts weren't refreshing enough, He chose and adopted us (see Eph. 2:4–5). We are *His* children. Part of *His* family. We are coheirs with Christ. "Consequently, you are no longer foreigners and strangers, but fellow citizens with God's people and also members of his household, built on the foundation of the apostles and prophets, with Christ Jesus himself as the chief cornerstone" (Eph. 2:19–20). Wow! Take a moment to meditate on that powerful truth. If you are God's child as a result of your choice to follow Him, then you are no different from Moses. So, whether your personal background offered all the benefits and opportunities of Pharaoh's household or you inherited a world of challenges, if you are God's child, then you are a daughter of the King! You have been chosen by Him, and you are one of His heirs.

If this chapter hits a tender spot, then it's time to reprioritize your history. Remember, overly attaching to anything in your origin or background will present a stumbling block in your perception of your self-worth. Today, remind yourself that your family tree has some giants of faith, giants like Moses. You are one of God's children, with power and purpose. Now it's time for you to leave a beautiful legacy—a legacy born out of an embracing of your true identity.

VICTORY VERSE

"For you created my inmost being;
you knit me together in my mother's womb.
I praise you because I am fearfully and wonderfully made;
   your works are wonderful,
   I know that full well."

PSALM 139:13–14

FREEDOM Q & A

1. What words would you use to describe your childhood? Your family of origin? Reflect on the words you used in these descriptions. What is your emotional response to seeing these words?

2. Consider your answers to the questions on the checklist. What specific innate characteristics or circumstances of your background have influenced your self-worth? How have they positively shaped your self-worth? How have they negatively impacted your self-worth?

3. How does Moses's story encourage you?

4. We discussed God's hand in your origin, your purpose, and your future. If you have trusted Him and made Christ your Savior, then you are God's child and a member of His family. How does this truth change your perspective and influence your self-worth?

5. List some of the heroes of faith mentioned in Hebrews 11. What is it like to consider them as a part of your ancestry? Your culture? Your family tree?

7

Who Is the Chief Thief?

A thief is someone who steals, a cunning enemy who sometimes presents themselves as if they will protect but instead takes advantage of an area of vulnerability. A thief desires to take what is not rightfully theirs.

It is important for us, as Christians, to acknowledge that we face a thief. Our thief, Satan, is not some random robber who is looking for a quick fix. No, this thief is a personal enemy, and we are his strategic targets. And unlike the occasional thief who regrets their behavior, Satan has no remorse regarding his attempts to steal. He was kicked out of heaven because he wanted to be God; he wanted to steal God's position. And he's been on the same pursuit ever since. No remorse. No repentance. He hates God. And, if you are one of God's children, he also hates you. He's not content with just stealing from you. He wants nothing more than to destroy you. This is warfare.

The Thief's M.O.

When police want to stop a thief, they study how he operates—his M.O. We need the same kind of information about our enemy.

What is his strategy, and what is his primary weapon? The good news is that he is pretty predictable. But let's not be naïve; he is also extremely sly. We shouldn't be surprised. He's a professional thief. And as I say often, "He only needs a crack in the door." Satan's primary point of entry is our minds. He gets into our head just as effectively as he did to Eve so many years ago. Satan's first documented lie was recorded in Genesis 3. Appearing as a serpent and described as "crafty," Satan questioned Eve: "Did God really say, 'You must not eat from any tree in the garden?'" (v. 1). Satan was setting a trap with an exaggeration and a trick question. He introduced the arts of leading questions and passive-aggressive communication in the first fourteen words he spoke to Eve. When Eve clarified that she could eat from any tree in the garden other than the tree in the middle (which would lead to death), Satan leaped at the opportunity to present God as a liar. "'You will not certainly die,' the serpent said to the woman. 'For God knows that when you eat from it your eyes will be opened, and you will be like God, knowing good and evil'" (vv. 1–5). Eve took the bait, believed the lie, ate the fruit, and suffered the consequences. What did she suffer first? Wouldn't you know it—insecurity. When she realized she was naked, she hid. Sound familiar?

So how does the enemy wage war against *our* minds? He does so in the same cunning and passive-aggressive manner that he used in the garden. He uses manipulation and deception to lead us to either doubt God or doubt ourselves. When he is not directly lying, he is using slivers of truth to exaggerate or minimize the facts. Let's never forget: any manipulation of the truth is a complete lie. And Satan is an all-out liar.

Satan fuels his mission with the weapon of comparison and commonly feeds on our feelings of inadequacy. Much like the piece of fruit he used to deceive Eve in the garden, he dangles in front of our faces things such as our appearance, our success, our need for approval, and our experiences in life. He swings these traps in front of us with the false promise that they define us. Most often his message is that we are not good enough. Occasionally, his message is that others aren't good enough. Satan convinces us that earthly things can make us either wonderfully whole or utterly and eternally broken. Neither is true. Too often, we take the bait, just as Eve took the fruit. If we believe the lie, then we're either puffed up with arrogance or in a pit of self-loathing. Emotional instability soon follows our taking the bait.

If we allow Satan to deceive us, then we rely on the opinions of others to shape our identity—other mortal beings who are subject to the same thief and the same misguided conclusions about their own value. We rely on our temporary successes or failures rather than our eternal purpose. We rely on our earthly roles and responsibilities rather than our eternal hope. We rely on our innate earthly characteristics rather than the promise of a new heavenly body.

Do you notice the theme? The enemy can only work on his turf—that which is temporary, earthly, and eternally meaningless. He cannot compete with God's position or the hope God offers, so he uses any crack in the door we give him and works to distract us, creating within us a tunnel vision regarding the here and now. As a result, we attach ourselves to things that don't really matter. Our appearance. Our success. Our need for the approval of others. Our roles in life. The color of our skin. Our age. The experiences of life. We get caught up in daily drama, daily routines, and false promises of how to make ourselves more valuable and more satisfied. We unintentionally, but naïvely, buy the lie and settle for a broken identity. And we don't even realize we've settled. The result? Feelings of insecurity, with emotional instability not too far behind.

Perception Is Reality

Remember, a thief is a robber. And our enemy desires to steal our worth. Since he can't actually take our worth, he focuses on shaping our *perception* of our worth. And as the old saying goes,

"Perception is reality," so we live life with a warped sense of what is real and true. A warped perception of reality leads to misguided emotions and behavioral responses. This thief has wreaked havoc through an *illusion*.

We can't sit around with no defenses to guard against a thief. Much like we wouldn't leave the front door unlocked or cracked open if we knew a dangerous person was outside, we must not sit idly as Satan plans his next move. We must respond, both defensively and offensively. Remember, Satan's point of entry is our minds. So, we must lock him out and fight him back. It's time for a quick lesson on fighting this not-so-typical thief.

How to Fight the Not-So-Typical Thief

The first step in fighting effectively is realizing we aren't in a typical battle. "For our struggle is not against flesh and blood, but against the rulers, against the authorities, against the powers of this dark world and against the spiritual forces of evil in the heavenly realms" (Eph. 6:12). We're not dealing with a thief we can see in the flesh. We're dealing with evil. A vicious attacker. Only with God's help can we take a stand. But, with God's help, we *will* be victorious! And here's how:

> Therefore put on the full armor of God, so that when the day of evil comes, you may be able to stand your ground, and after you have done everything, to stand. Stand firm then, with the belt of truth buckled around your waist, with the breastplate of righteousness in place, and with your feet fitted with the readiness that comes from the gospel of peace. In addition to all this, take up the shield of faith, with which you can extinguish all the flaming arrows of the evil one. Take the helmet of salvation and the sword of the Spirit, which is the word of God. And pray in the Spirit on all occasions with all kinds of prayers and requests. With this in mind, be alert and always keep on praying for all the Lord's people. (vv. 13–18)

When we are saved, we receive the protective armor described in Ephesians 6. We just have to put it on. We have the truth through God's Word, which provides us with discernment and direction. We have the righteousness of Christ, which covers us and allows God to see us as holy and blameless. We have the shoes of peace, which assure us that we belong to God as we step forward against the enemy. We take up faith, which gives us confidence as we face an unknown and unsettling attack. We pick up God's Word—we study it, meditate on it, and sometimes memorize it. And we pray. And pray some more, desperate for God.

But perhaps the most significant protection we must use in the face of insecurity is the helmet of salvation. Consider a football player who approaches the field. He's going to be hit. He's certain of it. His helmet protects his brain, but it's of no use if he doesn't put it on. Going onto that field without a helmet would be dangerous. What is that "helmet of salvation"? It sounds so abstract but is quite simple. It is the confidence of our salvation. The confidence that we are God's children. The assurance of our eternity with Him and our hope for the future. It represents the truth of who *He* says we are. This helmet is literally our protection from the enemy's false accusations. So how do we use the helmet? We simply measure any accusations, doubts, or destructive thoughts against what God proclaims to be true. This is where God's Word comes into play. How can we ever measure an accusation against truth if we don't know the truth?

Scripture says that the sword of the Spirit is the Word of God. A sword is a powerful, offensive weapon that stops an enemy in their tracks. And the Word of God is living. Powerful! "For the word of God is alive and active. Sharper than any double-edged sword, it penetrates even to dividing soul and spirit, joints and marrow; it judges the thoughts and attitudes of the heart" (Heb. 4:12). God's Word is *the* spiritual weapon for a spiritual war. And it will not leave you empty-handed when you are up against a powerful accuser.

So, when your thoughts are consistent with who God says you are, then celebrate and move on. But when they are inconsistent, you must take a different approach. You must agree with God. With truth. A helmet, by definition, prevents penetration. So you must use your helmet to prevent the penetration of a lie or a false belief that causes you to feel that you aren't good enough. Pretty enough. Smart enough. I like to think of an accusation from the enemy as being like a pebble that bounces off a helmet. It's not allowed any power to harm our minds. That is the kind of protection God has given us, and we must wear it and trust it if we are going to remain standing in this battle. Focusing our minds on the truth of our salvation and the whole truth of our identity provides unequaled protection from the enemy's attacks.

No Loitering

Jesus gave us a marvelous example of how to stand against this thief. As recorded in Matthew 4, Jesus was led into the wilderness, where Satan tempted Him. How did Jesus stand against Satan? Jesus used the Word of God and spoke back the specific truth that addressed the temptation. That's all Jesus said. He didn't let the conversation with Satan linger. He didn't entertain him with too much attention. He didn't loiter in negotiations or excessive dialogue. He just assertively and appropriately spoke the Word. And then it was as if He said, "This conversation is over." Jesus assertively resisted Satan, and Satan fled. We must do the same as Jesus did; we must assertively and appropriately use God's Word, avoiding excessive conversation regarding a lie. We must also resist Satan, with the confidence that he will flee (see James 4:7). And he will. Battle over.

Sister, if you are one of God's children, it's time to execute your authority. Put the enemy in his place. Your thief has a leash on him, and God is holding it. According to the book of Revelation, Satan's day of judgment will come, and Satan, "who deceived them," will be forever thrown into the "lake of burning sulfur," where he will be "tormented day and night for ever and ever" (20:10). You are an heir with *Christ*. You are *God's* beloved. And you have the *Holy Spirit* within you. You are in their hands—that's triple security against a thief. And you have access to the same power that raised Christ from the dead. But the enemy is causing you to struggle, with nothing more than the use of an illusion. A lie. A false belief. Have no more of it.

But I'm Not a Christian

Maybe you are not a Christian, and this discussion seems weird to you. Uncomfortable. Whether or not you are a Christian, the enemy will work to belittle your value in an effort to isolate you from God. His goal is to prevent your salvation. Don't think because you are not a Christian that this discussion doesn't apply to you. It does. Perhaps the enemy is just successful in separating you from God. In causing you to doubt God. In preventing you from trusting God for eternity. Or perhaps you are so convinced of your unworthiness that you won't even entertain the idea of a relationship with God. Maybe it's time to reconsider. Reach out to a trusted Christian friend or a pastor to discuss where to go from here. Salvation is simple. It just requires a decision to believe and submit. We're going to talk more about why God is worthy of that belief and submission in part 3. I hope you'll join me there.

VICTORY VERSE

"Be of sober spirit, be on the alert. Your adversary, the devil, prowls around like a roaring lion, seeking someone to devour."

— 1 PETER 5:8 NASB

1. How has the enemy caused you to doubt God? How has he caused you to doubt yourself?

2. How has Satan lied to you? How has he exaggerated or minimized truth? If you took the bait, what was the outcome of believing a lie?

3. How has Satan used the weapon of comparison to cause you to feel inadequate? Have you realized that the enemy was using an illusion, warping your *perception* of worthiness? If you have been living with this perception of unworthiness as your reality, what has been the outcome?

4. How might the helmet of salvation described in Ephesians 6 alter how you battle the enemy?

5. We discussed the example of Jesus in responding to an attack by Satan. Jesus didn't linger or loiter in conversation with the enemy. Have you given the enemy too much conversation? If so, how has this weakened you against his attack?

PART 2

UNNECESSARY PROBLEMS

I f your identity is not secure, then you have inadvertently invited and undoubtedly experienced some unnecessary complications in life. Why? Because your thieves have created false beliefs. And these false beliefs are powerful forces of destruction. The following chapters will address how false beliefs create specific, unnecessary challenges regarding your mind, emotions, and relationships as well as your spirituality and life development. After reading the chapters in this section, you will be able to identify the specific, preventable problems your insecurities have caused. These problems have likely wreaked havoc in your life and caused you great frustration.

The final chapter of this section focuses on the biblical example of an individual who created needless problems in her own identity crisis. As the saying goes, "Misery loves company," so we might all take a little comfort in finding that a woman in the Bible struggled with the same problems we wrestle with.

8

Mental

The problems created by our insecurities vary in nature. But they are always *unnecessary* problems. Sometimes these problems are relatively mild, perhaps so much so that others don't even notice them. Other times these resulting problems are horrendous, interfering with our daily functioning and quality of life. We're going to discuss the continuum of mental struggles and disorders that can potentially arise out of a false identity. Why do we begin with mental struggles? Because psychological pain related to insecurities is at the core of all the other struggles we face.

Satan is a liar and an accuser. His target is the mind—your mind. Lest we think this reflection is too theological, or just too abstract or irrelevant, let's have an honest personal discussion. You see, we all have an ongoing conversation in our minds. You and I both think thoughts throughout the day. Most of those thoughts we never acknowledge to another human being. We never speak them aloud. But they are there. And, left untamed, they are quite powerful. In fact, this private conversation may very well be the most important conversation any of us ever have. The irony is that the most significant conversation we have isn't even audible. The enemy is sneaky, isn't he?

In the mind of someone who is consistently psychologically healthy (which I'd dare say is only a portion of females), that internal conversation is sound, calm, accurate, instructive, biblical, and helpful. But in the mind of someone who has been robbed of a secure identity, that conversation is often loud, destructive, and cynical. The most common destructive thoughts I hear women report are "I am worthless," "I am ugly," "I am unloved," "I am different," "I am stupid," "I am inadequate," "I am not good enough," "I don't measure up," and "I can't do this." The enemy uses slivers of evidence to implant within us a destructive belief. Experiences of rejection. Past traumas. Failures. Feedback from others. Our own conclusions. Satan often weaves together the subjects covered in the first section of this book (things such as failure, approval, life experiences, or origin) to formulate an assault on our minds. The enemy lies, accuses, and exaggerates, and we take the bait. He often deceives with a fragment of truth that he then warps into an exaggerated form of the truth. Remember, anything other than complete truth is simply a lie. The result of believing a lie? We inadvertently team up with the enemy in a war against ourselves, with our minds being the battlefield. This is not a short battle. This is a persisting war that sometimes lasts for years. Sometimes for decades. Sometimes for a lifetime. The internal dialogue is not just destructive because it is *negative*; it is also destructive because it is *repetitive*. This kind of damaging internal dialogue is called rumination. Rumination is a powerfully toxic force, much like successful brainwashing, that literally shapes the brain and wounds the mind. We can't be naïve—an inaccurate but disparaging thought or a false humility is not passive. A false belief is aggressively dangerous.

All of us have our own unique dialogue. Think of what you say to yourself when you are encouraged or feeling hopeful. What are those specific thoughts? Now think about your thoughts on a dark day, when you are feeling down. What is your internal dialogue like then? What are your most familiar and repetitive thoughts? What are your toxic thoughts? If you have had years of rumination, these negative thoughts have become automatic and habitual. You don't have to work to think of them; they now grace you with their torturous presence without any invitation. Possibly even without you ever being aware. If they have shaped your identity, these thoughts are directed toward you as a person—and they have become a part of you. Second nature. If this is the case, it may take some genuine effort for you to accurately identify the destructive thoughts in your mind. But that is an important acknowledgment. So, look hard, be honest, and take the risk in confronting your thoughts. Be specific. Even write them down as you identify them, if you have the courage to do so.

Psychological Patterns

Those who struggle with insecurities often have specific thought patterns. Look over the following list of psychological patterns carefully. Perhaps you will notice some familiar patterns in your own life. This recognition is a powerful step in overcoming any negative consequences these patterns have caused. In addition, beware that any of these psychological patterns can lead to a chronic condition if they are left untamed and given power and credibility in your mind and life.

All-or-Nothing Thinking

The telltale sign of all-or-nothing thinking is the frequent presence of *always* and *never* in your thoughts. True, a few things in life are black-and-white, but a general pattern of thinking in absolutes indicates an exaggeration of the truth and is a sign that you have been conned by the enemy, who traditionally uses exaggeration as a form of deceit. This pattern of thinking can lead to thoughts of superiority or inferiority as well as a host of emotional struggles.

Example: *I always mess up relationships.*

Exception to the Rules

Those who struggle with insecurities frequently have different rules for themselves than they do for others, and they typically have no idea this thought pattern is present. These rules are related to grace and truth. For instance, while you may be quick to extend grace to someone else, you may have harsh thoughts toward yourself when you're in a very similar situation. Or you may be able to clearly and objectively see that a particular biblical truth applies to other people but not to yourself. This pattern of thinking creates self-loathing and is a deceptive tool of the enemy, who makes an objective truth something subjective. Ironically, given our conversation regarding all-or-nothing thinking, this pattern of thinking creates a gray area out of an absolute truth. If you struggle with being an exception to your own rules, you must remember that you too are human. You will make mistakes. You will sin. You can also be forgiven—just as everyone else to whom you extend grace is forgiven.

Example: *God could never forgive me for my past. I know with confidence that others are forgiven, but this is different. I am different.*

False Guilt

False guilt is identified by the presence of *should have, could have,* and *what if* patterns of thought. False guilt is the enemy's sneaky tool that results when we analyze the past unaware of his tainting. The conclusions from that past analysis are based on partial truths and/or partial theology and are therefore also peppered with false accusations. It is important here to distinguish between false guilt and conviction. False guilt is designed by Satan. Conviction is a tool of the Holy Spirit. This distinction is important, because you need to aggressively ignore one and aggressively listen to the other. False guilt, which results from taking blame for something that was not your fault, always leads to shame. False guilt can also be related to previous sin. I discuss more about this root of false guilt as well as the distinction between guilt and conviction in my book *Becoming Resilient*:

> Sometimes guilt is in regard to legitimate sin and regret, but it becomes false when we linger in the guilt long after we have repented and God has provided forgiveness. When we feel bad about our previous choices and are hammered by our guilt, we will do most anything to alleviate our negative emotions. But guilt is not of God. Guilt is an endless, unproductive motivator. Conviction, however, is of God and is evidence of the work of the Holy Spirit in guiding us to start or stop a certain behavior. Once we respond to conviction, the conviction releases. We can try to respond to guilt, but the release never comes. False guilt is an endless, relentless bully that will live with us the remainder of our lives if we allow it.[1]

I love how Robert McGee distinguishes guilt from conviction in his book *Search for Significance*: "Christians are freed from guilt, but we are still subject to conviction. . . . Guilt brings depression and despair, but conviction enables us to realize the beauty of God's forgiveness and to experience His love and power."[2] In essence, guilt attacks the person while conviction addresses behavior. If you notice a pattern of false guilt, you can begin working diligently to challenge your thoughts, preventing this pattern from becoming a chronic condition that creates chronic shame. Because guilt and conviction seem like abstract concepts and can easily be confused with each other, I challenge clients to use their hands in distinguishing between the two. Imagine one hand represents guilty thoughts from the enemy. Imagine the other hand represents conviction of the Holy Spirit. Then dissect your thoughts, one at a time, and imagine assigning them to a hand, either guilt or conviction. Notice which hand carries more weight. Are your thoughts dominated by guilt? Or conviction? Sometimes this simple, concrete exercise allows you to be more objective in making this powerful distinction and is a tool for relinquishing the false guilt that will keep you stuck.

Example: *What if I had left an hour earlier? That accident never would have happened. It's all my fault.*

Catastrophic Thinking

When normal levels of concern get turned up too high, catastrophic thinking results. This pattern of thinking is characterized by frequent ruminations on the worst outcome of any given situation. This pattern of thought creates anxiety and panic and can easily become a chronic condition if it is not challenged.

Example: *I was late for work today. I'm sure I'm going to be fired. And I'll never be able to find another job. This is awful. My career is ruined!*

Self-Doubt

Self-doubt is characterized by frequent internal questioning regarding your abilities or value. It can even be related to questioning your salvation or calling. It is a fixation on areas of weakness or critical feedback. This thought pattern creates fear and keeps you stuck. The enemy has been using the tool of doubt since the beginning of time, and it's one of his favorites.

Example: *I am not smart enough to do this. I may have misunderstood what I thought God was leading me to do.*

Racing Thoughts

Destructive thoughts easily lead to ruminations and can even become obsessive. These thoughts cause anxiety because they just won't slow down. Sometimes it may seem that you can't turn off the thoughts. They may become so distracting that you sometimes can't accomplish your daily tasks. You certainly can't lie down to sleep with peace and calmness. In fact, that's when the racing thoughts may really seem to kick in.

Example: *I feel like I am spinning out of control. I constantly think about what I've done wrong, what I have to do next, and how inadequate I am to do it. When I try to go to sleep at night, the thoughts get even louder.*

Comparisons

The most frequent tool the enemy uses is comparison. If this pattern is present in your life, then you find yourself frequently in dialogue with yourself about how you measure up against others. Strangers you see when you are walking through town. People you work with. Those you attend church with. Even your closest friends. When you are captured by comparisons, your conclusion is typically a sense of superiority (you are somehow better, prettier, more successful, etc.) or inferiority (you are not good enough, others are more blessed, etc.). Because God is not the author of comparison, this pattern cannot result in your appreciating the uniqueness of yourself or others. And though the pattern can be born anywhere—from the locker room to the church choir—it most frequently reveals itself these days in social media. If any social media platform creates a comparison pattern in your life, today is the day to deactivate your account.

Example: *She looks so pretty in that dress. I wish I looked like that. She looks like she has it all together. If I were more like her, I'd be happier.*

Self-Preoccupation

Each of the patterns above inadvertently leads to a self-preoccupied thought life. This doesn't necessarily mean arrogance. In fact, it's quite the contrary. Those who struggle with insecurities are generally so self-conscious that they have unintentionally become self-focused and have a false humility instead of a healthy humility. When we struggle with thoughts of unworthiness, we become cynically preoccupied with ourselves. Our self-loathing could even be considered self-absorption. The result? We find it difficult to notice the needs or wants of those around us. We may become disconnected and lonely, even among a crowd of people, because no space is left for others in our preoccupation with our own faults and inadequacies.

Neuroplasticity

Neuroplasticity means the brain is adaptable and changing. The bad news is that the brain can be harmed and physiologically impacted by our toxic thinking, particularly by thoughts of a repetitive nature. The good news is that the brain can heal as a result of consistently healthy and truthful thinking, suggesting that we have some power in changing our brains. Neuroplasticity takes our discussion regarding our negative thoughts to a new level of importance. If we want to be whole, we must be conscious and disciplined in our thought life. We cannot allow toxic thoughts to run amuck in our minds. We must submit not only our lives to Christ but also our thoughts about ourselves, allowing the Holy Spirit to direct our ideas and choices. This submission results in the rewiring of our brains and the renewal of our minds.

I wrote about this powerful concept in *Becoming Resilient*:

> Romans 12:2 has never been more relevant: "Let God transform you into a new person by changing the way you think" (NLT). Our brains are transformed when we, who know God and have access to the wisdom of God through the Holy Spirit, fully embrace the mind of Christ. "But we have the mind of Christ" (1 Cor. 2:16). Yes, we have the mind of Christ! So let's allow Christ to do a full reconstruction of our minds. Let's agree with Him rather than continue to hold on to destructive thoughts that are contrary to His Word.[3]

We must take this battle of our minds very seriously. The Bible tells us to destroy false beliefs and accusations against ourselves.

"We demolish arguments and every pretension that sets itself up against the knowledge of God, and we take captive every thought to make it obedient to Christ" (2 Cor. 10:5). This verse says to demolish anything that sets itself against the knowledge of God. I know you are thinking, *I am weak. How can I demolish anything?* Remember, God desires your freedom, and He will supply you with the power and discernment to demolish a false belief. God knows you. He knows your true identity. He knows who you really are. So, with His help, prepare to destroy anything that is contrary to His knowledge of you. How do you do this? First, you aggressively reject the identified lie. This rejection is often a concrete and repetitive exercise. For example, imagine putting your destructive thoughts in a prison cell, never to be released or heard from again. Or perhaps imagine them being erased from a chalkboard and replaced with a word of truth about yourself. Or imagine these destructive thoughts being deleted and replaced in the computer that is your mind. Use any and every image that works for you, and allow God to aggressively eliminate the repetitious cycle of negative thinking. With God's help and power, you can stop the assault against yourself, even if it has been an automatic process. Even if you're sometimes convinced the false beliefs are true. Even if you feel you are deserving of the assault against your identity. Even if the assault against yourself has been present for years. Even if it has been present for decades. It is never too late to become whole. And you can't be whole while believing a lie.

Imagine with me for just a moment. Imagine that as a child, you learned part of your multiplication table incorrectly. You repeated $2 \times 2 = 5$ over and over again. You wrote it on flash cards and took practice tests repeatedly until it became automatic recall. The problem? You memorized a lie. You've lived your entire life believing that $2 \times 2 = 5$. That has caused some confusion. What do you do? You must work doubly hard to reject the old, false equation and replace it with the correct one. You use flash cards.

You use repetition. You apply the same methods you used to learn the false multiplication. That would take a lot of work, wouldn't it? But without that hard work, you'd live the rest of your life believing an obvious lie: that $2 \times 2 = 5$. Much like recognizing that we've learned an incorrect multiplication equation as a child, we must identify our false beliefs, identify the corresponding truth, and then aggressively and persistently begin learning the truth. This learning of corresponding truth is the second step to mental freedom in the fight against insecurities. But since more is at stake than a false multiplication table, this step will also involve meditation. This will require that you not just repeat a corresponding truth but really imagine that truth being applied to your life. Ponder your acceptance of that truth. Allow that truth to play out in your mind like a movie, with the same attention and focus you've devoted to false beliefs.

These two action steps of assertively rejecting a false belief and then replacing that false belief with a corresponding truth using various tools of repetition and meditation literally change the pathways in the brain. Doing these things also results in measurable changes in emotional stability, which frees you from being stuck in a false identity. Unchecked destructive thoughts result in deep psychological pain and lead the way to additional unnecessary suffering. If the war against the mind is left untamed, it will create emotional instability, relational challenges, developmental complications, and spiritual disconnect. We'll address these issues in the chapters to come. But I want you to know it's possible to *prevent or overcome* these additional complications by aggressively addressing the war in your mind. Your psychological well-being depends on your attention to this battle. Don't give up the fight, and don't allow yourself to be complacent. Instead, let God transform and renew your mind. Why? Because the renewal of your mind mends your brain. A mended brain is a mended identity. And a mended identity is a mended life.

Psychological Problems

Everyone who experiences insecurities feels some level of psychological distress, but obviously not everyone who struggles with insecurities develops a problem that grows into a psychological diagnosis. When an individual's insecurities progress into an obsessive pattern, however, they become vulnerable to more severe psychological complications, such as anxiety disorders, mood disorders, body dysmorphic disorder, eating disorders, clinical depression, self-mutilating or suicidal ideation, conduct disorders, substance abuse disorders, and personality disorders.

Less common are those who are excessively attached to an inflated sense of self and whose obsessive patterns in that regard lead to narcissism. Their perception of their identity leads to arrogance, selfishness, and a sense of superiority to those around them.

Psychological problems like these negatively impact a person's daily functioning and require professional assistance. If a false identity has become deeply ingrained and obsessively patterned, and has resulted in psychological dysfunction in your life, please reach out for help. Your situation is not hopeless, but your struggles have probably become chronic and have taken a toll. It is possible to live a more stable and psychologically healthy life. Reach out for help, and do it soon, before these patterns steal any more precious time. Healing is possible, and you will most successfully achieve it with the professional assistance of someone who is trained to facilitate your recovery.

Psychological Resilience

How do we bounce back from the mental struggles related to our insecurities? Let's look at a biblical character to find some strategies for resilience. Most of us can identify with Moses. God called him to do something he felt utterly inadequate to do. He felt that he wasn't a good enough leader, he feared making mistakes, and he had a stutter that made him self-conscious when he spoke to others. His identity was wrapped up in his thoughts about himself—specifically, his thoughts of unworthiness. But God's view of Moses was radically different. He saw Moses as having innate value and had created him for purposes that were intimidating to Moses.

God called Moses to become a leader for the nation of Israel, to be one of the most influential persons of the Old Testament. But Moses didn't want anything to do with that call. He felt completely ill-equipped to lead a nation of people against someone like Pharaoh. Moses's insecurities immobilized him. He was afraid he couldn't accomplish this task. He was afraid others wouldn't understand that this task was God-ordained. He was afraid those he would lead would not believe him and therefore would not respond to his leadership. Mostly, he felt inadequate to speak with poise and confidence to that many people. In fact, Moses pleaded with God to use someone else. Anyone but him. "Who am I that I should go to Pharaoh and bring the Israelites out of Egypt?" (Exod. 3:11).

God's answer to Moses is very important—because it also applies to us. "I will be with you" (v. 12). After resisting more, Moses finally accepted that God intended to use him and agreed with God about moving forward. Once Moses made this shift and accepted God's call, he began to bounce back, and his self-worth became something more significant than simply his thoughts of his own personal inadequacies. His worth became shaped by who God defined him as being. And even more importantly, his worth became shaped by his personal dialogue with God and the assurance that God was within him.

Our psychological resilience develops from the acceptance of God in us and with us, and from our innate value in accomplishing His purposes because He is the One accomplishing them through us. If we minimize our value, we minimize the value of God in us. And He cannot be minimized.

It's time to start bouncing back. Take back the identity that never should have been stolen from you and gain the "sound mind" that comes with the mind of Christ (2 Tim. 1:7 NKJV). If God is with you, let your thoughts be His. God can rescue you from your mind's relentless battles. He can protect you from the assault against your worth. He can shield you from the exaggerations, comparisons, and unfounded conclusions regarding your value that have gripped and immobilized you for years. Yes, He can revive your identity and make you secure, but it must be on His terms. Terms of truth. Nothing more. Nothing less.

You *can* think differently. Begin to routinely talk yourself through truths, transforming your thoughts. Speak in the quietness of your mind, or literally speak out loud things like, "God can make me whole." "God wants me to be secure and free." "It is God's desire that I see myself the way He sees me." Focus on a few phrases and Scriptures of truth that are easy for you to remember and that point you to freedom. Repeating and meditating on these truths will make them familiar. They will transform your mind. I know, the enemy is telling you right now that this is crazy. That this kind of recovery can't be yours. But self-doubt like this has created many issues for you before, and it has probably never paid off. Try the route of faith today. Trust that God can make you whole, and even bring you to the place where you're okay with being whole. Secure. Free. It's not too good to be true. It's just different. Embrace something different today as God paves the way for your rescued identity.

VICTORY VERSE

"For God has not given us a spirit of fear, but of power and of love and of a sound mind."

2 TIMOTHY 1:7 NKJV

1. What are your familiar, destructive thoughts (your negative thoughts and ruminations)?

2. Can you imagine life without the presence of these thoughts about yourself? What difference would their absence make? (Remember, with perseverance in taking these thoughts captive, they will begin to weaken.)

3. Are you impacted by the presence of any of the psychological patterns described in this chapter? If so, which ones? What has been their impact?

4. Do you struggle with a chronic psychological condition? Or a psychological diagnosis? Do you feel your insecurities have impacted this vulnerability in any way?

5. Addressing the psychological distress connected with insecurities requires agreeing with God about your value. About your identity. What is your innate value? Who does God say you are?

6. Take an objective view of yourself, as if you are gazing at someone else who has the same experiences, lives with the same challenges, and is offered the same grace and love of God. What would you say to her about her value?

7. How does the discussion regarding neuroplasticity apply to you? How does God nudge you concerning the toxicity or health of your thoughts and mind?

9

Emotional

Y ou've heard the term "hot mess." We sometimes use that phrase when our emotions are getting the best of us. So, in this chapter, we're going to talk about another complication of insecurity—a genuine hot mess of emotional chaos and why women might be extra vulnerable to it.

Examination of the brain reveals that in females there is more connectivity between the hemispheres of the brain, particularly the frontal lobe.[1] Women also have greater cell density in the frontal lobe. Why are these facts significant? Because the frontal lobe is the brain's emotional control center. There are various other differences between men and women in the structure of the brain, blood flow, and hormones. And these combined differences give us females the beautiful ability to think intuitively. To have a "gut feeling" about things. They also aid us in reasoning and impulse control as well as in transitioning relatively easily from task to task.[2] They allow us greater empathy for others and award us strengths in emotional intelligence.

But with every strength comes vulnerability. And the same strengths that provide our emotional intelligence can also make us vulnerable emotionally, susceptible to a hot mess if we're not careful. Remember, any strength turned up too high can create chaos. When turned too high, our gut feelings, our empathy, and our ability to connect one situation to another (rather than automatically compartmentalizing experiences) can lead to comparisons and ruminations—the perfect ingredients for insecurities. The irony is that our strengths can become our biggest messes.

I have long felt that insecurity is the most significant struggle of women in America. But while we are discussing some differences in the genders, I will share that I have also observed lust to be a common struggle of men in America. This is just my personal observation. But isn't that a combination of struggles straight from the enemy's camp? Nothing feeds insecurity like the threat of your man looking at another woman. Indeed, Satan is a relentless villain, and he preys on our weaknesses. That's why it is so important that we recognize our weaknesses regarding our insecurities and work to overcome them.

While insecurity may not be the presenting problem of most clients who walk through my door, I typically discover it somewhere in the mix. The presenting problems are typically more emotional in nature, which brings us to the subject of this chapter.

We all experience powerful emotions. Overwhelming emotions. The emotions derived from our insecurities create massive complications and confusion.

Emotional Complications of Insecurity

A variety of emotional complications can develop as the result of a broken identity. These are the emotionally related concerns that bring clients to my office for their first session. These are discussed here in no particular order, as they can display differently in people.

Anger

Furious. Boiling. Red hot. Raging. These are words we use to describe the intimidating emotion of anger. Because anger can be such a dominant emotion, it's important to understand that it is a secondary emotion. This means that prior to feeling angry, we feel a silent, primary emotion. Much like peeling a layer of an onion, we can peel back anger and discover something rawer underneath. These primary emotions are more vulnerable. One primary root of anger is inadequacy. Anger shields us from more vulnerable primary emotions, which is why we are subconsciously drawn to that secondary emotion. This explains why when we are challenged or feel that we don't measure up, we may take a defensive stance. Anger is a less vulnerable emotion than inadequacy, so it will often be the most prominent emotion that others see in us.

Let's clear up a few misconceptions. Some people are very afraid of anger. They equate it with violence and sin. But anger, as an emotion, is not sinful in and of itself. It is our behavioral response to anger that can potentially be sinful. "In your anger do not sin" (Eph. 4:26). Anger is a tricky emotion because it is our most powerful emotion. In fact, it is so powerful that it is incredibly effective when used righteously against injustice. In treatment, when I am helping a client who is fighting an addiction or eating disorder, I will sometimes work to entice anger in them because they need the effective fuel of this potent emotion when working against such a powerful force. But in life in general, we have to handle anger with kid gloves because it can make some serious messes. It is the most difficult emotion to manage, and it is the most likely emotion to result in a sinful response. That unhealthy emotional response is the one we are concerned about in the context of our discussion today. When a response is destructive, I would describe this as unhealthy anger.

Unhealthy anger can be directed inwardly, so that no one else sees it (anger toward self, which leads to self-loathing). This form of anger can leave us susceptible to depression and self-harm. Unhealthy anger can also present as spoken or violent outbursts, such as verbal or physical assaults, road rage, or temper tantrums. Unhealthy anger can also lead to a more passive-aggressive response, which is a manipulative anger response. The silent treatment is an example of a passive-aggressive display of anger. All these responses to anger are destructive. They complicate our relationships and compromise our testimonies. Left untamed and unresolved, anger can also lead to bitterness—one of the other emotional complications we will discuss in this chapter.

Anxiety

When we have thoughts of inadequacy and struggle with insecurities, we also feel excessively self-conscious. Our self-awareness gets turned up too high. We feel as though others can somehow see through us, that they can view our faults and weaknesses. We feel exposed. Awkward. Scared. We're conscientious about our appearance, what we say, our posture, and our mannerisms. When our self-awareness gets turned up too high, it develops into insecure self-consciousness, creating significant anxiety. Those who experience a general state of anxiety typically experience mild, uncomfortable physical symptoms. Those who suffer a more acute experience of anxiety, a panic attack, experience a cascade of more intense, and sometimes disabling, physical symptoms.

How do you know if you're experiencing a panic attack? Your body will tell you. You'll notice symptoms such as shallow and rapid breathing or difficulty catching your breath (like you're hyperventilating), chest pain, sweating, stomach pain or diarrhea, shaking, dizziness, or tingling. You feel an urgency to escape whatever situation you are in. Anxiety can feel very scary. In fact, for some, it feels like a heart attack and leads many people to the emergency room. If you experience these symptoms, make sure you see your physician to rule out more serious contributors, but if the diagnosis is indeed anxiety, be assured that it cannot hurt you.

But let's not be naïve; anxiety is a strongly *perceived* threat. It is so strong a perceived threat that we will do nearly anything to eliminate the symptoms. The most common thing we do to eliminate anxiety is what I call "shrinking our world." Because we want to avoid an anxious response, we withdraw and begin avoiding people and places to protect ourselves from the effects of anxiety. Unfortunately, this response provides no protection at all and only increases anxiety and further limits our opportunities to live an enjoyable life. In summary, anxiety is an emotional response to insecurities that complicates our lives and limits our joy.

Sensitivity

When our intuition and self-awareness are turned up too high as a result of our insecurities, we can also become highly sensitive. Harmfully sensitive. We may become easily embarrassed and self-conscious. We may also become overly analytical of our surroundings and interactions with others. We may scrutinize their verbal statements, their nonverbal cues, what they said, what they didn't say, their tone of voice, their posture, and additional dynamics of our interactions with others. This heightened analysis easily leads to our feelings being hurt by others, even when they have no intention of hurting us. We take things personally when they are not meant to be personal at all. This heightened sensitivity complicates our lives, challenges our relationships, and robs us of joy. It fuels even more negative and destructive internal thinking and ruminating, which then can leave us vulnerable to the next emotional complication: depression.

Depression

Depression is one of the most commonly diagnosed mental health disorders in America.

There are many different types of depression. Some forms are almost entirely physiological in nature, precipitated by a vitamin deficiency or chemical or thyroid imbalance. Other forms are more situational in nature and are highly impacted by our circumstances and internal dialogue. This is the form of depression addressed in this section. Specifically, depression that is born out of insecurity.

How do you know if you are depressed? You may experience fatigue, apathy, a desire to isolate yourself, and an atypical lack of motivation. Even the things you once enjoyed may have lost their appeal. Nothing seems to bring you joy. You may experience changes in your eating habits (eating for comfort and gaining weight, or loss of appetite and weight loss). You may experience changes in your sleep habits (sleeping throughout the day to escape emotional pain, or challenges with insomnia due to racing thoughts). Depression, when at its most severe, leads to feelings of hopelessness and can even result in suicidal thoughts.

Depression resulting from insecurities and destructive thinking can cause significant undue suffering, with ramifications to our psychological, physical, and relational well-being.

Envy

We live in a culture of comparisons. When we struggle with insecurities, we compare ourselves to others and often come to the conclusion that we don't measure up. We then believe the lie that our lives would be better, and we would be more valuable, if we had the experiences, the bodies, the jobs, or the relationships that other people have. We look to other people as a standard, leaving us vulnerable to envy. Envy is a common, often hidden and embarrassing, emotional response born out of these comparisons. When envious, we are deceived by the "grass is greener syndrome" and genuinely believe that other people have a better life. We gaze on their lives, sometimes obsessively. We want what they have. This envy drives either withdrawal or competition, and therefore prevents us from being able to authentically connect with others. It may prevent us from being able to genuinely celebrate the successes and joyful experiences of others and may subtly cause us to hope for their failure so we will feel better about ourselves—so that we'll feel less insignificant. This complicating emotional response robs us of joy and can also ruin relationships when left untamed.

Shame

Shame is perhaps the most heartbreaking emotional response. When regret of any form is turned up too high, it develops into a deep and degrading sense of unworthiness. Self-disgust. A feeling that we are undeserving of the basic love or respect of others. Shame is a powerfully painful emotion that leaves us with a lack of love and respect for ourselves. A sense of incompetence. Humiliation. A belief in our inability to be forgiven. Shame, unchallenged, is an unnecessary emotional complication that creates significant suffering and anguish.

Bitterness

Unresolved and unaddressed insecurities, comparisons, sensitivities, and jealousies are the perfect ingredients for the ultimate recipe of bitterness. Anyone can develop a bitter or disagreeable spirit, even if we direct it only toward ourselves. Before we know it, we are experiencing a chronic form of cynicism and criticism.

Bitterness of this kind shapes our life experiences. It's as if all our life encounters—even the sweet moments—go through a filter of cynicism and are tainted by a "bitter taste." We evaluate through the lens of criticism rather than gratitude. Untamed bitterness will not heal with time alone. In fact, unaddressed bitterness will simply keep us stuck. We have all seen grumpy—and old—people. It's exhausting to live life with a bitter taste. It ages us. And it spoils the joys of life, creating unnecessary disappointments, struggles, and sufferings.

How Emotions Control Us

This discussion is so relevant because our emotions will automatically control us if we allow them to do so. And, if we are not intentional in *preventing* their control, they will rule us and run our lives with the power of a zealous but untrained and out-of-control automatic pilot.

Think about it. What happens in the life of someone whose anger makes decisions for them? Or whose anxiety makes decisions for them? Or whose envy makes decisions for them? Or whose sensitivity makes decisions for them? Or whose shame makes decisions for them? Or whose depression makes decisions for them? Or whose bitterness makes decisions for them?

Destruction. That's what happens. The result is more than an emotional mess. It's a mess of massive proportions that impacts all areas of their life.

Destructive Behavioral Responses to Our Complicating Emotions

Just as our thoughts lead to our emotions, our emotions lead to our behaviors. And destructive thoughts that lead to destructive emotions will certainly lead to destructive behaviors. Destructive behaviors include stealing, lying, gossiping, having emotional or physical affairs, excessively shopping, gambling, or abusing alcohol or illegal substances. Destructive behaviors also could include settling for an abusive relationship, or self-harm through an eating disorder, cutting, or attempting suicide.

All these destructive behaviors represent an attempt to escape, medications for the pain of insecurity. But they are false escapes and poor substitutes that only lead to additional pain and suffering.

What Do the Scriptures Say?

The Scriptures speak to the issues of the heart. And we certainly need a word on this subject. Here's a humbling thought: "The heart is deceitful above all things and beyond cure. Who can understand it?" (Jer. 17:9). Our "gut feeling" is like a single indicator light in our car. It can give us information, but we still have to sit in the driver's seat and pay attention to all the other indicator lights and what is happening in our surroundings. That one indicator light is not our pilot. Likewise, we can take note of what our emotions indicate, but we have to use many other judgments if we are going to function healthily. And we must remember that many of our emotional responses are misguided and exaggerated.

I am comforted by God's Word regarding our own self-loathing. I have a feeling you need to hear it as well: "If our hearts condemn us, we know that God is greater than our hearts, and he knows everything" (1 John 3:20). God's truth is greater than our turned-too-high intuition. And when our emotional response condemns us and leaves us feeling even more insecure, it is He who we must trust. He's almighty God. Omniscient. All-knowing. He knows more than our frontal lobes! And, friend, He's wiser than our occasionally misguided, self-condemning conclusions.

How to Manage Our Vulnerable Hearts

Scripture also speaks about how to manage our hearts. "Trust in the LORD with all your heart and lean not on your own understanding; in all your ways submit to him, and he will make your paths straight" (Prov. 3:5–6). We have to trust God and submit our emotions to Him. What do we get in exchange for our submission? He will straighten out our emotional mess. Feels like a weight will be lifted from us, doesn't it?

"Above all else, guard your heart, for everything you do flows from it" (Prov. 4:23). We must take a defensive stance with our emotions. We must be on guard. Yes, our ability to connect with others, our intuition, our empathy—all these things are important. And we don't want to turn them off completely; that would be like turning off an important indicator light in our cars. But we must also *guard* our emotions, ensuring they are not turned too high. We must be aware of our vulnerability to their messes. And we must make sure we give them only the power to *guide* us, not to *control* us.

Gaining Stability

If you are experiencing any of the emotional complications we've discussed in this chapter, then you are probably exhausted. Overwhelmed. And these negative emotions cause you to feel even more insecure. You may even feel like you are going crazy. You're not alone. Let's discuss how to gain emotional stability.

When we find ourselves in an emotional mess, we are desperate for stability. We don't want our emotions controlling our lives. But where do we start?

We must start with our thoughts. Why? Because our emotions are born directly from our thoughts. Our destructive emotions are born directly from our destructive thoughts. In contrast, healthy emotions are born of healthy thoughts. Emotional stability is found only in truth. So we must first discipline our thoughts if we want to discipline our emotional messes.

How? Measure your thoughts against God's Word. If your thoughts are consistent with His truths, then keep repeating those thoughts. But if a thought is inconsistent with God's truth, reject it. It is just that simple. And just that tough. This requires deliberate and intentional effort. It requires work—but work with great dividends. We're going to discuss this more extensively in the final section of this book.

Tips for Maintenance

Some other important tips for maintaining emotional stability include exercising regularly, journaling, getting sufficient sleep and rest, relying on social supports, and practicing healthy nutrition. If you continue to struggle emotionally, make sure you see a doctor to evaluate any potential medical issues that may be exacerbating your difficulties.

VICTORY VERSE

"If our hearts condemn us, we know that God is greater than our hearts, and he knows everything."

1 JOHN 3:20

FREEDOM Q & A

1. We discussed various emotional complications of insecurities. Which emotional complication do you experience with the most prevalence? What have been the effects/outcomes of this negative emotional experience?

2. In what ways have you noticed your emotions have control in your life? What has been the impact of their control?

3. Reread the victory verse. Is it possible that your heart is inaccurately condemning you? God is wiser than your heart. What does He have to say about your self-condemnation?

4. Emotions, when operating according to God's design, are effective indicators. With that said, what is your emotional response to this chapter? What does this response indicate?

5. Even more importantly, what does God speak to you following your reading of this chapter? (Remember, your heart is a potentially effective indicator, but He is wiser than your heart.)

10

Relational

The essence of the Christian life is living in relationship with God. But, as followers of Christ, we are also members of the body of Christ. We're born to live in relation with other people. To be connected. "Now you are the body of Christ, and each one of you is a part of it" (1 Cor. 12:27). We're not designed to live as lone rangers.

God designed our relationships for a purpose. "A friend loves at all times, and a brother is born for a time of adversity" (Prov. 17:17). "As iron sharpens iron, so one person sharpens another" (Prov. 27:17). Our connections with others are to be good for us and good for them. A strengthening of one another that can only be accomplished by supporting and rubbing off on one another in a healthy and biblical way. Peter gave instruction for how we are to respond in relationships. To keep a relationship healthy and God-honoring, Peter coaches, "Finally, all of you, be like-minded, be sympathetic, love one another, be compassionate and humble" (1 Pet. 3:8). That's a tall order, isn't it? Consistently presenting these characteristics to others to whom we relate can be difficult at best. Developing and maintaining healthy relationships can be a challenge. And this is particularly true for those who struggle with insecurities.

We all struggle with at least some insecurities. That is normal this side of heaven. And those mild insecurities have only mild effects on relationships. But more significant insecurities can have more significant impacts. Frankly, that hot mess we talked about in the last chapter can result in some serious and tangible messes in relationships. How? Remember, our destructive thoughts lead to destructive emotions. And these destructive emotions lead to destructive responses. These destructive, insecurity-driven responses often show up in real life through our relationships, creating dysfunctional dynamics. Insecurities can strain or even destroy a perfectly good relationship or leave us vulnerable to an unhealthy relationship.

My Personal Experience

For years, my personal insecurities authored my relationship choices. Perhaps they have done the same in your life. The most prominent evidence of that destructive authoring in my life was in my dating relationships. I remember dating a guy who I was confident God didn't want me to date. I tried my best to convince him to become the type of man I thought God would want me to be with. My boyfriend would have nothing of it. Not only were my boyfriend and I unequally yoked, but we also had an emotionally destructive relationship. So how did I respond? Did I leave? Did I quickly walk away and instead trust in God? Nope. I stayed. Why? Because I was terrified. It wasn't that I was afraid of being without this *particular* man. It was that I was afraid of being without *any* man. Alone. Being alone would emphasize my sense of unworthiness, and that was an additional vulnerability I was not prepared to bear.

I stayed until God put me into a corner. In an encounter with God one evening that was completely undeniable to me, I sensed Him saying, "Choose this day whom you will follow: him or Me?"

With God's help, I responded with obedience and finally broke away from the idolatry of that destructive relationship and made an intentional choice to follow God.

Unfortunately, my insecurities were still an open wound. And I was accustomed to medicating that wound with relationships. I began bouncing from one date to the next. Don't get me wrong. These were not bad guys. On the contrary, I dated some good guys. Even a few wonderful and godly gentlemen who were respectable and kind. But the problem was that I continued to date when I knew God was calling me to "fast" from dating. God was wooing me to Him *alone* so that He could heal me without distractions. I knew that. But I resisted. Once again, I was scared. I was afraid to be alone. My insecurities got the best of me. As a result, I hurt some good and undeserving guys who were probably misled by my willingness to date them. My insecurities had previously created additional suffering for me. This time, my insecurities invited confusion and suffering into the lives of innocent people in my path. Insecurities are not victimless, and they can invite all kinds of unnecessary chaos and pain into relationships.

Examples of Relational Chaos

Everyone is vulnerable to experiencing a degree of insecurity. But when insecurity becomes more severe and camps out too long, it creates relational chaos. Let's look at some of the more serious dysfunctions that are present when our insecurities are heightened and projected onto our relationships. If you struggle with chronic insecurity, you are going to find some familiar territory below. Ask God for discernment on this issue and to help you be honest with Him—and with yourself.

Neediness

It's tough being insecure. It's scary and uncertain. And this uncertainty can cause us to become dependent on others to feel okay about ourselves. We feel that we need the approval and reassurance of people, so we cling to those who provide these things. However, when we are needy, we cannot be reassured. We may have difficulty making decisions and rely on others for guidance, advice, and leadership. As a result of this dependence, an unhealthy and lopsided pattern develops in the relationship. Essentially, one person becomes the helper and the other person becomes the helpee.

If we are needy due to our insecurities, we may feel anxious when our helper is too distant or panicky when we are concerned about their potential abandonment. This anxiety and panic can fuel more desperate reactions, sometimes even resulting in our *creating* situations in which our helper will be needed. We may fail to respect their boundaries. We may even manipulate situations to force our helper to remain close and ensure they do not leave.

Neediness born out of insecurities causes us to depend on others for our emotional stability. Our needs become bottomless pits that define the relationship and serve as a reason to keep the other person close. Unfortunately, this relationship dynamic often invites the very thing that scares us most: abandonment. Our neediness can cause the other person to feel that they are walking on eggshells. As a result, they back away. Confide less. Ultimately, they may come to a point at which they can no longer invest in the relationship because they are exhausted.

Over time, neediness creates a chronic seriousness in a relationship. It starves the joy of living life with another person and robs the relationship of fun and laughter. This is why healthy individuals cannot maintain a close relationship with someone who is exceedingly needy. The helping dynamic puts tremendous pressure on them, and ultimately drains them and drives them away. If you notice this pattern in your own life, be cautious. Another individual cannot assume the sole responsibility of carrying you emotionally. If they stay close despite your neediness, it is an indication of their codependency and their own need to be needed. But if they are emotionally healthy and your excessive neediness continues, they will have no choice but to create a boundary. Neediness is an example of how insecurities create additional, unnecessary pain in individuals and in relationships. If this pattern of neediness is taking place in the context of a marriage, you may need some professional assistance to facilitate healing in your relationship.

Codependent Caretaking

A codependent relationship is a dysfunctional helping relationship. Insecurities can drive us to take on a role in a relationship in which there is potential for us to be the hero. In the role of helper or caretaker, we are drawn to those who are struggling, and our way of thinking and responding within the relationship is wrapped up in that person's needs. In fact, we suppress our own needs in an effort to meet their needs. But those needs may be a bottomless pit, and we are ill-equipped to meet them.

In the beginning of the relationship, we may become excited when this needy person shows appreciation for rescuing them. But this excitement is really just self-medicating a deep sense of unworthiness. The excessive need to be needed, characterized by codependency, leaves us vulnerable to excessive tolerance of destructive patterns. For instance, when unable to effectively help the other person, we might stay in a relationship defined by addiction or domestic violence. We may find ourselves constantly adapting to try to meet the person's perceived needs. We compromise our stand against drugs to keep them calm. We take them to the casino despite our dislike of their gambling addiction. We tolerate their violent mood swings. Our intention is never to enable, but our fear of losing the relationship creates an enabling dynamic that fuels the dysfunction in the other person.

In a codependent relationship in which we are the helpee, we will often feel more like a parent than a partner. We give. And they take. We avoid conflict but use passive-aggressive approaches to express our frustrations or resentments. We rarely say no. We stay even when doing so is harmful for us. We cover for the other person and make excuses for their behavior. All this is in an effort to avoid abandonment, the greatest relationship fear sparked by insecurities.

Toxic Jealousy

Our insecurities can be so dominant that they fuel jealousy. Mild jealousy may just cause us to feel even more insecure. But toxic jealousy will create much more destruction and disease in our relationships. Jealousy becomes toxic when it creates a crisis in a relationship. For example, toxic jealousy can lead to our being controlling of others. We may not want them to have other friends or interactions. We may feel threatened when they interact with their family, old friends, or new acquaintances. We may press to know where they are at all times, or harass them with questions, or accuse them of betrayal because we are paranoid of their interactions with others. We may even become abusive. Domestic violence is often linked to deep-seated insecurities and toxic jealousy. When we have toxic jealousy, we become so absorbed in our own pain and needs that we cannot recognize the pain our interactions create in the life of another person. Our toxic jealousy is poison, sometimes constructing a dangerous relationship filled with suspiciousness and paranoia.

Remember, destructive thoughts lead to destructive emotions. And destructive emotions lead to destructive responses. If you can relate to the experience of toxic jealousy, then your thoughts have brought disaster into your relationships. If you want to be whole, and you want your relationships to be whole and healthy, you must get some help so you can sufficiently address this concern. Don't allow toxic jealousy to plague another relationship. In fact, your only hope for a healthy relationship is to address the insecurities that are authoring your destructive choices. It's time to take up the fight against your real enemy—your own toxic jealousy—and determine not to be robbed of another opportunity for a healthy and satisfying relationship. Your actions hurt. Those you are hurting deserve something more. And so do you.

Isolation

The last type of relational chaos that we will discuss is more unique than the previous types. Isolation is the *withdrawal* from relationships—the absence of genuine connectedness. When we are insecure, relationships can be intimidating. We may feel that we are unworthy of meaningful relationships. Or we may be unsure of how to relate to others. Even for those of us who are innately extroverted, insecurities can cause us to feel shy and can create a degree of social anxiety.

Relationships also represent the potential for rejection. They require risk. And when we are insecure, that risk is sometimes too overwhelming. So we may avoid getting close to others to prevent pain. We may keep others at a safe distance through superficial relationships and abandon potentially meaningful relationships when a person gets too close. "I'll hurt you before you have a chance to hurt me" becomes our subconscious pattern of protection and self-preservation. Insecurities cause our guarding to be excessive and destructive. We long for healthy connections with others and may even dislike our pattern of isolating. Sadly, we sabotage the very thing we desire and unintentionally invite additional pain.

Evaluation Time

If this chapter hits a tender spot for you, then you may want to honestly evaluate your relationships. Why? Because the dynamics of your relationships may be feeding additional insecurities. And additional insecurities mean unnecessary additional pain.

If you can relate to any of the above examples of relational chaos, then at least some of your relationships (or isolation from them) are further increasing your insecurities. Are you in a relationship with a man who has poor boundaries with other women? Do you have genuine evidence that he is cheating on you? Does he call you names, insult you, or put you down? Does he intimidate or manipulate you? What about a relationship with a friend? Is there high conflict in your relationship? Does your friend take advantage of you? Gossip about you, with no consequences? Give you the silent treatment if you don't respond as she likes? If you can answer yes to any of these questions, then you are in a destructive relationship.

There are many examples of destructive relationship characteristics, and these are just a few, but you get the idea that they cause a high-stress, walking-on-eggshells dynamic that is exhausting and anxiety producing. A destructive relationship can occur in any context. It can occur with a family member, a friend, a colleague, your boyfriend, or your spouse. Your insecurities have perhaps created vulnerability in a specific relationship. And now your destructive relationship is triggering additional insecurities and suffering. You won't be able to heal until you place boundaries within this relationship.

A boundary doesn't have to be permanent, but it must remain long enough to interrupt the unhealthy patterns. I know this sounds scary. But it's true. This relationship, as it is currently, will keep you stuck in your insecurities. If this paragraph describes you, and particularly if it is a marital relationship that concerns you, I urge you today to make arrangements to meet with a trusted mentor, pastor, or counselor. You don't have to make any major decisions today. You don't have to do anything different right away (unless you are in physical danger). You just need to make the single decision to reach out for guidance.

Boundaries

If you have identified insecurities as having a negative impact on important relationships in your life, then now is the time to begin making some adjustments—before that impact becomes even more significant.

Where do you start? Boundaries.

If insecurities have created neediness, then as your identity heals, you can also stretch in your relationships. That means allowing a healthy boundary between you and others. In a practical sense, that means slowing down your automatic response to rely on another person. Practice making some decisions on your own. If the time you spend with another person overwhelms them, then practice using some of that time to take a trip to the gym or volunteer at your church. Allow those relationships that are important to you the space to breathe and to be healthy. I like to think of healthy relationships as a dessert, and I often share this with clients: "A healthy connection with another person is the *icing* on the cake. Not the cake." Your husband or friend or family member cannot replace God's presence in your life (the cake). But they sure can add to the pleasure of life (the icing). A healthy relationship is one that you are not desperate to have but that you fully enjoy.

If insecurities have created codependent caregiving, step back and consider where a healthy boundary needs to be. If you are enabling something dysfunctional in another person, then you are not doing them any favors. And you may be allowing yourself to be wounded in the meantime. Consider your situation as if it were not your own. Can you envision what a healthy boundary would look like when you take an objective view? What responses would you find appropriate for someone else in the same situation? Be as objective as possible, and reject any responses that cross the line. In a practical sense, this may mean you cease to cover for someone else. Or you say no when no is really the healthiest answer. It may mean you allow yourself some space to breathe, and you focus on taking care of some of your own basic needs that have been neglected for some time.

If insecurities have created not just mild jealousy but toxic jealousy, then a healthy boundary will likely involve a "relationship fast" so that you can seek some direction about the relationship apart from the chaos. Don't look at a relationship fast as a lifelong commitment to separate. This can be overwhelming. Rather, look at it simply as a fast from contact for a week. During that week, assertively refuse all contact and give yourself and the other person space to determine what boundary will be necessary. Whether you are the giver or the recipient of the jealous responses, a relationship fast is in order. If you are experiencing toxic jealousy within a marriage, then it is time to reach out for professional help as you seek wisdom about strategies for healthy boundaries.

Finally, if insecurities have shrunk your world and caused you to isolate yourself, then it's time to reevaluate your boundaries. You have likely enforced boundaries that are too restricting in an effort to prevent pain. But boundaries should be designed to allow for adjustment when necessary. And as you gain freedom from your insecurities, you will discover the opportunity to stretch these boundaries.

If establishing boundaries is confusing to you, don't hesitate to seek counsel. Professional counselors are experienced in guiding individuals through instituting boundaries, and you will likely benefit from the input of a trusted Christian counselor.

The Rest of My Story

Earlier I shared my personal story regarding insecurity, and how it negatively impacted my relationships. I think it is fitting to tell the rest of that story. I am so grateful today that I finally trusted God with His leading. I indeed "fasted" from dating. During that season, I had a genuinely wonderful time. I grew closer to Christ. I took pleasure in the relationships with my Christian sisters in a way I never had before. I also enjoyed healthy fellowship with male friends whom I never dated. God was healing my insecurity and making me whole. It felt wonderful and freeing. I finally experienced genuine contentment in my relationship with God that prevented me from needing any other "medication" to help ease my insecurity.

Ironically, it was after this season that I met my husband, a man whose integrity and walk with God would have so intimidated me before that I never would have considered dating him at all. I would have felt too unworthy and undeserving of being in relationship with him that I wouldn't have even considered dating him. But thankfully I did give him consideration. And, now, nearly twenty-five years later, I'm sure glad I did!

My willingness to trust God with my insecurities and relationships radically altered my future. I cannot adequately verbalize my gratitude to God for how He healed that brokenness in my life and mended my ability to live freely in relationship with others. That experience was significant in preparing me for God's call to Christian counseling. I knew what a radical transformation looked like. And I knew other people deserved to experience that same kind of freedom. So I responded with obedience. This time, with no hesitation or resistance. I invite you to join me, with no hesitation or resistance, as God woos you to a safe, loving, and healthy relationship with Him. Therein lies freedom from your insecurities, my friend.

VICTORY VERSE

"As iron sharpens iron, so one person sharpens another."

— PROVERBS 27:17

FREEDOM Q & A

1. What is your personal story? How have your insecurities affected relationships in your life?

2. We all will experience at least some degree of insecurity this side of heaven. This insecurity, mild or significant, has a

similar degree (mild or significant) of impact on our relationships. What level of impact would you say your insecurity has had on relationships in your life? How has this cost you or invited additional pain?

3. Can you identify with any of the relational chaos traits discussed in the chapter (neediness, codependent caretaking, toxic jealousy, or isolation)?

4. If insecurities have had a negative impact on important relationships in your life, what boundaries might be appropriate? Where might you start implementing these boundaries?

11

Developmental

Insecurities cause all kinds of hurts. And those hurts can occur at any age or stage of life. In fact, insecurities can even oppress and complicate our life development. They can potentially cast a shadow on how we progress through various stages of life as well as how we maneuver the challenges that come with each stage.

Child Development

Young toddlers have an innocence of life. They love themselves. They are comfortable in their own skin. A toddler can gaze at her naked body in the mirror with a smile. She can dress in a tutu, hold a plastic microphone, and sing a song at the top of her lungs with grand confidence. She doesn't yet know to feel insecure. We're all born with that accepting assurance. But as the developmental cycle progresses, we lose it somewhere along the way. I've met with many individuals who developed depression, anxiety, or an eating disorder in late adolescence, who can look back to their elementary years as the introduction to the insecurities that paved the way to their struggles.

A heightened sense of unworthiness can be triggered by any number of things in childhood, including life events, traumas, and even temperament. About 50 percent of school-age kids are living in divorce situations, single-parent homes, and/or blended families.[1] These arrangements can often leave a child feeling uncertain and insecure, not just about themselves but about their environment. Of course, abuse or trauma in childhood will feed a sense of unworthiness as well. But even temperament can influence self-worth as early as childhood. Our biologically determined, God-designed temperament can influence our vulnerability to insecurities and therefore also impact our personal development. Temperament determines how we process life. Therefore, children with laid-back, easygoing temperaments may be more resilient in bouncing back from some of the triggers of unworthiness. Similarly, those with sensitive temperaments may be more vulnerable to the same set of triggers. (But before we get caught up in the old nature versus nurture debate, let's remember that God has created us wonderfully and perfectly, and He has provided everything we need to heal and thrive. We just need to be aware of the vulnerabilities that come with our unique design.)

Insecurities in childhood can impact various specific areas of development. Here are just a few brief examples. Insecurities can, for instance, stifle a child's *creativity*. They may also influence *speech development*, causing anxiety-driven delays and exacerbating speech disorders. Insecurities can be a cause for and a result of a condition such as stuttering, which occurs primarily in children. Insecurities can also contribute to delays in *social development*. Trauma-driven insecurities can inhibit attachment, which drives a wedge in relationships from the time of infancy. In addition, children who struggle with feeling that they don't measure up may have difficulty learning to interact socially with adults or to resolve conflicts with peers. Children are still figuring out how to identify and process emotions; insecurities may compromise the natural flow of their *emotional development* and their ability to manage life's inevitable negative emotions. These same personal uncertainties may also cause a delay in the normal progression of *independence*, because a child who feels insecure may not feel capable of taking on the world independently. They may instead doubt themselves and cling tightly to a parent or caregiver. Lastly, it's in this period of childhood that a person's personality is formed and therefore also potentially influenced by insecurities.

Consider Jane, a fourth-grade student whose temperament is naturally more extroverted but whose insecurities cause her to present as someone introverted at school. Her thoughts and feelings of inadequacy show up in the classroom, where she is less likely to volunteer to provide answers to questions and ask questions when she is unsure of an assignment. Her insecurities cause her to withdraw from peers. Jane's grades suffer, and she falls between the cracks academically, which ultimately impacts her learning and academic development and further exacerbates her feelings of inadequacy.

Adolescent Development

Central to the adolescent stage of life is the transition from childhood to adulthood, separation from parents, and entry into independence. This is a tricky season, at best, and almost everyone battles insecurities. The innocent assurance of childhood is long gone, and adolescence is a vulnerable, and often intimidating, season of life. For some, it is a time of identity crises. Hormones. Acne. Changes to the body. Drama with friends. Drama with guys. Figuring out a style. Trying to decide what to do beyond high school. Identifying beliefs about sexuality, politics, and God. The pressures to conform are intense, and peers typically have more of an influence than adults during this developmental season. Adolescence is a perfect storm for insecurities.

Ideally, adolescence is a time for identifying personal strengths and accepting personal weaknesses. But these important self-realizations may be complicated for someone who struggles extensively with insecurities, because their insecurities cause them to excessively focus on weaknesses and minimize strengths. This complication prevents them from being able to make an honest evaluation as they explore potential future roles in life, which is critical in *identity formation*.

Adolescence is also a time for the development of *body image* and *sexuality*, both of which can be warped by a false sense of self. This leaves insecure teens vulnerable to either withdrawing from dating relationships or excessively depending on those relationships. This developmental stage is also a time when young people sharpen their *social competence*—they develop comfort with skills such as eye contact, self-expression, working effectively with other people, and speaking fluidly with others. Insecurities inhibit them from thriving in social competence, creating instead a vulnerability to social anxiety and withdrawal from potentially healthy peer relationships. Those who struggle with insecurities may also be more likely to succumb to peer pressure in their teens, inviting regrets that could potentially plague them for years and provide additional ammunition for the enemy to attack their self-worth.

My observation is that adolescents who have a healthy sense of their personal identity tend to manage negative emotions and situations more effectively and with increased resilience. Teens who feel good about themselves are more likely to take initiative and work diligently in school, to participate in extracurricular activities, and to relate with other peers socially than those who do not feel good about themselves. Likewise, those who feel inadequate are more likely to withdraw from peers and school activities and may give up on tough academic or extracurricular tasks too quickly compared to teens who feel comfortable with themselves.

It is during this adolescent period that a person's identity is formed, making it a crucial life stage. True or false, healthy or unhealthy, that identity is carried into adulthood, where it leads the way in shaping relationships, decisions, and responses to life's circumstances. Consider Isabelle, a sixteen-year-old sophomore in high school. She is a beautiful young girl who thrives in school but struggles with body image. When her body started to change a year ago, she became ultra-self-conscious, often comparing her body to that of her peers and rarely feeling that she measured up. She is keeping up her grades, but the rest of her life feels as though it is in shambles; she's striving for control. She has begun restricting her food intake and occasionally purges in an effort to reach a body weight that she feels will allow her to feel better about herself. What she doesn't realize is that her identity is broken, and in an effort to repair her hurt, she is inviting a destructive disorder that may last into adulthood.

Adult Development

By the time of young adulthood, many individuals have developed committed and intimate relationships. The majority of females marry sometime in their twenties and start families relatively soon after that. After one or two decades, these same females may find themselves sandwiched between caring for their children and caring for their aging parents. Finally, they reach a season of aging themselves, learning to cope with the challenges of growing older.

Young adulthood is symbolized by a season of significant and life-altering decision-making. Careers. Relationships. Beliefs. A young adult who struggles with insecurities will feel significant anxiety in this stage, because decision-making of this magnitude is extremely challenging in the face of self-doubts. A young adult who has low self-worth may tend toward continued isolation or detachment rather than commitment in intimate relationships.

A young adult who wrestles with insecurities may struggle with commitment in other relevant areas of their life as well. They may hold back from obtaining further schooling because they fear failure. They may refuse to set goals or set goals that are under the threshold of their potential. They may bounce back and forth between potential career options. Insecurities can further bleed into their work life, directly impacting their motivation, drive for achievement, and willingness to take risks. They may procrastinate on completing important applications, interviews, or projects. Even if their spiritual gift is leadership, they may hesitate to make important decisions or struggle with the responsibility of problem solving, conflict management, or supervising the tasks of other people. These patterns directly impact the progression of their career development and are due to the anxiety fueled by insecurities.

During *middle adulthood*, people experience a natural season of reevaluating life and beliefs, of exploring and desiring to achieve purpose in life through meaningful work and relationships. Those who have a healthy identity can maneuver this season rather well, with a productive response that sharpens their focus in preparing for the second half of life and leaving a legacy. However, those who struggle with insecurities will experience this stage more harshly. Rather than making adjustments that fit more purposefully with their life goals, they may become stuck in shame over time they regretfully spent. Or they may respond in panic, sometimes making radical and shocking changes, such as abandoning their career or family—thus the term "midlife crisis."

Late adulthood is a reflective time as well. It is a time of managing the aging of the human body and accepting the mortality of life. It can be a season of giving back, mentoring, passing on traditions, and leaving a meaningful imprint on the next generation. Those who maneuver this stage healthily do so with a focus on purpose, allowing them to experience peace. Those who struggle with insecurity also struggle with purpose, so they meet this stage of late adulthood feeling despair rather than peace. It is an unfortunate season for those who struggle with a false identity, as this despair even further complicates the challenges of aging and death.

Consider Sarah, a woman in her forties. Sarah lives and works under a glass ceiling, imposed not by other people but by her insecurities. She withdraws from risk and snuffs out potential career opportunities because she feels unworthy and is afraid of failing. She settles for staying in a job she despises because she fears exploring something more challenging. She feels such regret about not having already done something more purposeful. Now she feels it is too late and lives with much sorrow.

Spiritual Development

Spiritual development is even more crucial than all the other aspects of development, particularly for us as Christians. After we make a decision about God and trust Him for our salvation, we experience a progression in our continued trust of Him. We mature and go about the process of making Him Lord and placing our faith in Him, not only for eternity but also for life this side of eternity. In essence, we can go from infancy to adulthood in the context of our faith in God. This development is exemplified in the maturity of our prayer life, in growing in the knowledge of God through the study of Scripture, and by learning to yield to Him through the many good and bad seasons of life. We mature as we experience life situations that reveal evidence of the existence of God and His activity in our lives. These situations fertilize our trust that He is indeed who He claims to be. And when we come to maturity in fully believing that God is who He says He is, we also mature in accepting that *we are who He says we are.*

We can imagine how insecurities are a stumbling block to spiritual development. Due to feelings of their own unworthiness, many people reject Christ altogether. But insecurities also inhibit us as Christians. If we struggle with feelings of unworthiness, we will feel unworthy before an all-knowing God. If we struggle with inadequacies, we will hide from an all-perfect God. Though none of us are deserving of Christ's sacrifice, insecurities will lead us to reject the opportunity to live life relating to Him. We won't feel worthy of that gift or His presence in our lives. Shame will create an unnecessary boundary between us and a beautiful relationship with a loving God. Apart from that ongoing relationship, we will experience no spiritual growth. We will remain infants who trusted Him for eternity but never took our first steps as toddlers.

The outcome? We live independently from God. Lonely. Without hope. Struggling for purpose in life. Without the benefit of His guidance, love, or comfort. Without His protection or instruction. Because we feel He should surely reject us, we reject Him. We may also reject His church, feeling unworthy to be part of the body of Christ or to receive the blessings of being part of a local church.

The enemy targets no other developmental context more than our spiritual development. Sure, he relishes the destruction of our minds and emotions or difficulty in our relationships, but nothing causes Satan to rejoice more than our separation from God. And insecurities are just one of the tools he uses to create that invisible barrier.

Physical Presentation

While insecurities may not directly and significantly impact our *physical development*, they certainly can impact our *physical presentation* at any age and stage of life. Insecurities can lead us on a quest for a perfect appearance, but they can also work in the opposite manner. Did you know that low self-worth even impacts things as basic as hygiene? If I don't value my body, I may be careless about it. I am less likely to nurture it, to take the time to present myself nicely, or to wear clothes that modestly embrace my acceptance of my body. I may not shower daily. I may not even look in the mirror to be aware of how I am presenting my body in public. I may dress sloppily or wear dirty clothes, even when I have the resources to do otherwise. I may show no interest in proper nutrition or the health of my physical body.

This lack of attention to self-care, at any stage in development, invites harassment by those who are looking for a target, which can trigger even more insecurities within us. I'm not suggesting embracing an arrogant physical presentation or an unhealthy attachment to appearance. But I am suggesting that a broken identity can present itself in this most basic developmental aspect of hygiene and self-care. When we take care of our bodies, we experience a natural boost to our mood. A workout, a healthy meal, a warm shower, or a set of clean clothes feels great, as do a pedicure or a new hairstyle. It is normal for us to enjoy these simple pleasures in life. But when we are developmentally stunted in this area, we are robbed even of those simple, superficial joys.

Arrested Development

The phrase "arrested development" simply means that something has us stuck in a previous stage of development, and even as adults, we respond to life as if we are still in that earlier stage. This is why, for instance, you and I have both met individuals in their thirties or forties who act more adolescent than middle aged. They may display childlike behavior, such as temper tantrums, selfishness, or decision-making struggles.

Insecurities (invisible stumbling blocks) certainly can play a role in fueling this stagnation. A false identity stunts growth because it allows for minimal self-efficacy in various aspects of development. We feel ineffective and inadequate to progress through life. Ironically, any type of arrest in adult development further heightens insecurities, as there are expected spoken and unspoken societal milestones for each stage of life. The good news? By definition, arrested means "temporary," so we can bounce back from our stunted growth.

Consider also the impact of drugs on arrested development. Our development becomes stalled at the point when we began using the drug, and development remains stifled until we no longer use it. If you are struggling with a false belief regarding yourself, then insecurities are the drug that is stunting your growth. You can quit that drug right now and begin growing again. You don't have to remain stuck developmentally because of low self-esteem, self-worth, self-efficacy, or whatever term you want to call it. Resilience is yours. And it's time to live. To enjoy living. And to enjoy the person God has created you to be—with all the milestones of life that can be celebrated!

VICTORY VERSE

"Before I formed you in the womb I knew you."

— JEREMIAH 1:5

FREEDOM Q & A

1. If you highly value God's role in creating you, you are more likely to bounce back from momentary struggles with self-worth and move through normal development. On the contrary, if you minimize the value of God's role in creating you, then you are stunted, because you can't see the value of your purpose. Embracing value and purpose is required for healthy development. How much do you value God's creation of you?

2. How have insecurities impacted you across your life span? How do you feel about this impact to your development?

3. Though insecurities may not have touched your physical growth, they can impact your physical presentation. How has this been demonstrated in your life?

4. How have insecurities robbed you of spiritual development? Where would you like to be in relation to God?

5. Have insecurities arrested your development in any way? If so, how? (Remember, by definition, arrested means "temporary." If your answer to this question is yes, then it is time to start bouncing back.)

12

Sarai

If the previous chapters have spoken to you regarding your struggle, then let me assure you that you are not alone. Insecurities have been making royal messes in people's lives since the beginning of time. No one is exempt. Not even the very first female ever created, who lived in a perfect garden. Not even one whose name is timeless and whose descendants make up the most extraordinary family tree in the history of humankind, including none other than Jesus Himself. Let's look at Sarai, an Old Testament example of how insecurities can lead us to make crazy decisions in our lives and how false beliefs regarding our worth can create some incredibly complex predicaments. If Sarai came to my office for a counseling session and told me her story, this chapter reflects how I'd interpret her experience.

If you've spent any time in a church, you'll likely recognize the names Sarai and Abram (whose names God later changed to Sarah and Abraham). Abram is known throughout the generations for his faith, which was "credited to him as righteousness" (Gen. 15:6). When Abram had a vision and heard that from

Sarai's aged and infertile body they would have a child, he believed. When he was told that child would have as many off-
spring "as the stars in the heavens," Abram believed. Even in
a situation that didn't make sense, Abram believed. Even in a
circumstance that was contrary to his expectations, Abram still
believed. Abram's belief doesn't mean he didn't make bad decisions.
Nevertheless, we remember him as a man of faith. When we remember Sarai, though, we tend to think less about her faith and
more about her insecurities. Let me explain why.

An Infertile Woman

We're introduced to Abram and Sarai in Genesis 11, and we
learn more about Sarai's childlessness in Genesis 16. Though
the Scriptures don't specifically state this, one could reason-
ably conclude that Sarai's identity would have included being
a mother. Sarai undoubtedly struggled with her identity as a
childless woman in a society that measured a woman's value by
her fertility. The emotional and spiritual challenges of infertility
created in Sarai what in today's terms could be referred to as
an identity crisis. I imagine her childlessness monopolized her
thoughts. She probably compared herself to other women who
were mothers and fantasized about what it would be like to be
a mother herself. She likely wrestled with feeling inadequate
and broken. One thing we know for sure, Sarai put aside her
relationship with God, blaming Him for her childlessness (see
Gen. 16:2). Her desire to bear children led her to a desperate place, a place in which she was unable to trust or wait on
God's promise that He would make her husband "a great nation" (Gen. 12:2). Out of fear that her childlessness would last
forever, Sarai put herself in the driver's seat of her life, with no
thought about where the road might lead and who might get
hurt in the journey.

How Sarai "Resolved" Her Crisis

How did Sarai "resolve" her crisis? Weary of waiting on the ful-fillment of God's promise to Abram, Sarai sought another option to produce a child. She offered her servant, Hagar, to Abram. It was an accepted custom in those times for a man to produce an heir through a concubine. So Sarai instructed Abram to sleep with Hagar as a way to build a family through her.

In her attempt to solve her immediate problem, Sarai created several new ones for herself and those around her. Hagar indeed conceived a child, and immeasurable conflict and turmoil soon followed. Hagar despised Sarai. Sarai's jealousy of Hagar grew to an all-time high. Sarai suffered emotionally and acted out by responding so abusively toward Hagar that Hagar fled into the wilderness. Marital dissension and resentment resulted between Sarai and Abram. Ishmael, the son of Abram and Hagar, would bring additional strife. Sarai grew to hate the results of her ma-nipulation. Insecurity had surely made a mess.

A New Name for a New Identity

Something exceptional happened in Sarai's life. Did God ignore His promise because of Sarai's disobedience and the mess it caused? No. God was gracious to Sarai. In fact, He gave her a new name. A divinely appointed name. A name symbolizing His promise to bless her. God changed her name from Sarai to Sarah. Sarah means "princess." It was a new name for her new identity as "the mother of nations." This was the first time God specifically promised to make Sarah a mother. Generations of kings would come from her lineage, culminating in Jesus, the Messiah King.

Also, God, as a sign of His covenant with Abram to make him the "father of many nations," changed Abram's name to Abraham (see vv. 4–6). But Sarah and Abraham were not the only ones in history to whom God gave new names. Sometimes in the Bible when God did something significant in someone's life, it was accompanied by a name change. For example, Saul experienced a name change. As did Jacob and Simon. You perhaps more readily recognize them as Paul, Israel, and Peter.

Can you imagine what that must have felt like to receive a new name from God Himself? Today, in many parts of the world, a bride takes the last name of her groom, demonstrating their marriage covenant. I recall how strange and awkward it felt early in my marriage whenever I introduced myself to someone with my new name. I was accustomed to my old name—the one I'd carried for more than two decades. But my awkwardness didn't cancel out my new name. And now that new name is just as natural to me as if it has always been mine. Perhaps Sarah, Abraham, Paul, Israel, and Peter each experienced this same awkwardness after their name changes. But they ultimately accepted the transition nonetheless.

Reflecting on the new names God gave to these faithful followers causes me to ponder a time in my life in which I was also assigned a "new name." In the latter years of my college experience, God did wonderful things in my life and for my identity. Insecurities were healed to the extent that they can be healed this side of eternity. It was a beautiful time of peace and anticipation in my life. Unrelated, but coincidentally, at this same time, friends on campus randomly assigned me a new name—Lou. It wasn't a name of symbolic meaning or spiritual significance. It was just a fun nickname. Because it was assigned to me at a pivotal point in my life, I embraced it as a symbol of the wonderful things God was doing in my life. Healing me. Guiding me. A new name brought a fresh and simple joy.

Sometimes we take on a false identity and a mistaken name, forgetting that God uses our messes but doesn't identify us by them. Never have I seen it recorded that God changed someone's name to "mess," despite all the documentations in Scripture of messes they might have made. Let's be sure that we don't mistakenly name ourselves. Instead, let's rely on God to give us our new name. A "new name that the mouth of the Lord will bestow" (Isa. 62:2).

Maybe God has never divinely spoken a new name over you. Maybe friends have never given you a nickname. But consider the name God might speak over you as He heals your brokenness. A new name that is symbolic of a new identity. A name perhaps known only to you and God. A name that brings you fresh and simple joy and reminds you that you are His prized child. Look with anticipation for the name God may reveal that symbolically represents your healing and acceptance of your innate value. Write down that name at the end of this chapter. Then embrace that name and allow its recollection to refresh and encourage you.

Bringing It Home

Sarah fell victim to the thieves we identified in the first part of the book: appearance and comparisons, success and failure, approval and rejection, life experiences and trauma, roles and responsibilities, background and origin. If only she could have believed the truth about herself. Think of how much unnecessary pain she could have prevented.

Sarai was so determined to produce a child that she was willing to take extreme measures. She was wrong. Just like you and I have been wrong. The guy. The career. The diet. The new car. There are many substitutes for wholeness. And when we attach our identity to them, they transform into tools the enemy uses to rob us of joy. Sarah's quest to bear a child distracted her from a healthy identity. You and I can look to Sarah as an example from which we can learn. You see, we all have our own insecurities, and they make no less a mess in our lives than Sarah's insecurities did in hers.

God Keeps His Promises

But before we get too hard on Sarah, or ourselves for that matter, let's reflect on a few additional facts regarding her story that will be encouraging for us to remember. First of all, Sarah possessed a strength that is worth noting. She was the faithful wife of the "father of many nations." Despite his obvious weak spots, Abraham still had incredible faith, and God labeled him as righteous. Sarah was Abraham's right hand, and she faithfully followed him as he sought to the best of his human ability to follow and trust God. Yes, her insecurity created a few messes. But in some areas of her life, her faith overshadowed her struggles. How encouraging!

And, finally, at the ripe age of ninety, Sarah received the gift she had longed for through the decades. God fulfilled His promise, and Sarah bore Isaac (see Gen. 21:1–2). Sarah experienced the joy of motherhood that she had so desperately wanted. We can imagine that the last thirty-seven years of Sarah's life were full of primarily love and laughter.

So remember: even when our insecurities get the best of us, even when we make horrific messes in our lives, God is still faithful. If God can use someone like Sarah, He can certainly use you. Thank Him for that, and allow that divine purpose to overshadow your struggles.

That is a hope that bears exceedingly great joy.

VICTORY VERSE

"You will be called by a new name that the mouth of the LORD will bestow."

— ISAIAH 62:2

1. Put yourself in Sarai's situation. How might she have felt as an infertile woman in her society? How might this have impacted her self-worth? In what ways do you relate to her struggle?

2. Sarai fell victim to all the thieves we identified in the first section of this book. Consider how she may have been vulnerable to each of these thieves.
   - Appearance and comparisons
   - Success and failure
   - Approval and rejection
   - Life experiences and trauma
   - Roles and responsibilities
   - Background and origin

3. How does Sarai's desperate attempt to resolve her insecurities speak directly to you?

4. Sarai made a mess with her insecurity-driven panic. How can you relate?

5. Sarai received a new name—a sacred and divinely appointed name—following her messes. How does this truth encourage you?

6. You were challenged to consider the name God might speak over you as He heals your brokenness. A name perhaps known only to you and God. A name that reminds you that you are His and that brings you joy. Write that name below.

_____

7. Sarah bore Isaac at the ripe age of ninety. God faithfully fulfilled the promise that she had longed for most of her life. How does this fact speak to your situation?

—— PART 3 ——

THE NECESSARY SECRET

Part 2 is like a punch in the stomach, isn't it? Our insecurities have created so many messes. So many unnecessary problems and sufferings. Thank God that our stories don't end there. You see, there is a way out. There is freedom from the oppression of our insecurities. There is a necessary secret. And the remainder of this book is devoted to exposing that secret to freedom.

In the following chapters, we'll meet the Audience of One and show why He is worthy of our dependence. We'll discuss the practical benefits of living with a secure self. And in perhaps the most important chapter of the book, we'll learn all about the Formula for Wholeness and discover its transformative power in our lives. We're also going to meet a young woman who successfully implemented the secret to freedom and experienced wholeness despite competing threats to her identity. You will be inspired and refreshed by her example.

Friends, your rescue mission awaits. Go, accept your freedom.

13

Audience of One

So many clients have said things like this to me:

I've tried everything. I've dated all kinds of guys. Some great guys. Some not so great guys. I've had a successful job, making good money. I've climbed that corporate ladder. I've managed to sometimes be accepted by the popular crowd. I've worked and worked to get the body I thought I had to have. You know, I experience a feeling of elation occasionally when something really works out. But it doesn't last. It is so short-lived. And the letdown from that outcome is nearly unbearable. Nothing gives me what I am after. I just want to feel okay with myself. I've never experienced that. Maybe when I was a young kid—but certainly not since then. How am I ever going to get there? Is it even something I should hope for?

Most of us have been on a quest at some point in our lives to just feel okay with ourselves.

But if defeating all the thieves we've discussed in previous chapters isn't enough, then how do we find some peace within our own skin? Is there any way to heal our insecurity? Can anyone provide a permanent solution to our broken self-worth? I know—you're tired of false promises. You're tired of expecting something great and then being let down. You're tired of the disappointment and the emptiness.

There really is a Person, and one Person only, who will give you what you need and won't rob you of a thing. No more stealing your joy. No more unnecessary struggles. No more messes. There is an Audience of One who will be sufficient for your journey. No more looking to everyone around you for acceptance and approval. No more looking for ways to *earn* a healthy self-worth. That Audience of One is God. And God alone.

All Your Eggs in One Basket

"You're saying I have to put all my eggs in one basket. That is scary. What if He is not enough?" Many of my clients express this hesitation. And we're going to spend some time in this chapter considering why God is worthy of our dependence regarding our self-worth. "For now," I tell my clients, "let's just acknowledge that nothing else has worked. In fact, *everything* else that you have tried has eventually robbed you and left you feeling even more empty, shamed, and inadequate." This reality check is enough for most clients to be willing to consider the risk of putting all their eggs in one basket. Yes, one basket. One audience.

Characteristics of Our Audience of One

An Audience of One simply means we depend on God for our self-worth. We shift our focus from many audiences to a single audience. And since that is a pretty radical recommendation, it's time now to consider who God is, and if dependence on Him is even a good idea. Then, assuming you agree that relying on Him for your self-worth is what you've been needing, we're going to consider what He has to say about your self-worth so you'll know what to believe about yourself. Here are some characteristics of God that make Him the perfect provider.

Stable

God never changes. *Never.* The Scriptures tell us He is the same now as He used to be, and He'll continue to be the same forever into the future. According to Hebrews 13:8, "Jesus Christ is the same yesterday and today and forever." If you've been living on a roller coaster, you need stability. God is not here one day and gone the next, though His presence may be more strongly felt at certain times than others. He is perfectly constant and unchanging. He never changes His mind. Depending on Him for your self-worth will bring the stability you crave. No more artificial highs followed by very real lows.

Wise

God is all-knowing. Yep. He knows everything. Everything. "Oh, the depth of the riches of the wisdom and knowledge of God! How unsearchable his judgments, and his paths beyond tracing out" (Rom. 11:33). He is wise beyond wisdom, and He has never made an error. Nothing is hidden from Him. There are no mysteries to Him. Therefore, dependence on Him is a wise choice, and one that brings with it even greater wisdom and discernment.

Safe

God is all-loving. He loves you perfectly, even when you feel unlovable. No abuse. No manipulation. No strings attached. No conditions. In fact, He loves even when it requires great sacrifice: "For God so loved the world that he gave his one and only Son, that whoever believes in him shall not perish but have eternal life" (John 3:16). His love for you cost Him something precious. He is a giver, not a taker. He loves completely and fully. He loves loudly. How does He love so safely and perfectly? Because He is holy. Without sin. Without agenda. Imagine the impact of accepting His radical love. He'll also allow you to reject Him. He is a gentleman and will not manipulate you into depending on Him.

Merciful

Despite God's holiness, He extends grace to us in our humanness. God forgives. Grace is a gift He provides freely. We can't earn it. And we don't have to. We just have to receive it. "All are justified freely by his grace through the redemption that came by Christ Jesus" (Rom. 3:24).

Protective

God's commands are boundaries for our protection. They provide security. In addition, His angels offer a buffer against potential tragedies, and His Spirit offers comfort for experienced tragedies. He is the author of justice. He rights our wrongs.

> I lift up my eyes to the mountains—
>   where does my help come from?
> My help comes from the LORD,
>   the Maker of heaven and earth.
> He will not let your foot slip—
>   he who watches over you will not slumber;
> indeed, he who watches over Israel
>   will neither slumber nor sleep.
> The LORD watches over you—
>   The LORD is your shade at your right hand;
> the sun will not harm you by day,
>   nor the moon by night.
> The LORD will keep you from all harm—
>   he will watch over your life;
> the LORD will watch over your coming and going,
>   both now and forevermore. (Ps. 121)

Relational

God is not a detached creator. He didn't just make you, and now watches you from afar. He created you specifically for His pleasure, giving explanation to the fact that He is an interacting Father, brother, and friend. He is tuned in. Engaged. He loves to communicate with you. And He desires to live life with you, allowing you to experience His presence in your daily life. "God did this so that they would seek him and perhaps reach out for him and find him, though he is not far from any one of us. For in him we live and move and have our being" (Acts 17:27–28).

Sovereign

God is in control. "Are not two sparrows sold for a penny? Yet not one of them will fall to the ground outside your Father's care" (Matt. 10:29). Given all the other attributes of God we've discussed, it's comforting to know that God, so pure, wise, and trustworthy, is also in control. Complete control. You can safely release the reins because He already has them. You've just been wearing yourself out.

God Is Unusual

Stable, wise, safe, merciful, protective, relational, sovereign. Have you ever met anyone like Him? I've seen people who have a couple of these characteristics, but not all of them, and certainly not to completeness or with everlasting consistency. And I've never met another human being who had an ounce of divine sovereignty. God is unusual. There is no one else like Him.

God's character evokes my trust. Understanding His attributes frees me to make Him my Audience of One. Furthermore, if I can trust Him and trust that He is who He says He is, then perhaps I can also trust that I am who He says I am. Could the same be true for you? Can you imagine trusting Him to be who He says He is and then trusting His description of you to also be fully accurate?

While you are pondering that question, why don't we take the time to discover exactly what God has to say about your identity.

Who Am I?

I want you to consider your darkest days. The days when you struggle the most with who you are. Days when you are inhibited by feelings of inadequacy. On those days, who do you say that you are? Take the time to write out a short list of your answers in the form of an "I am" statement.

After you've finished your list, set it aside. We have another assignment to complete.

If God is a trusted judge and an accurate reporter of truth, then I'm interested in His opinions. How about you? Let's look at who He says you are. According to His Word, if you know and have trusted in Him, then He claims you as His child, His friend, and His heir. You are accepted and forgiven. You are chosen. You are His masterpiece! Consider just a few of His descriptions of you in the format of another set of "I am" statements:

I am His child (see John 1:12).

I am a friend of Jesus (see John 15:5).

I am forgiven, justified, and redeemed (see Rom. 3:24).

I am not condemned (see Rom. 8:1).

I am a fellow heir with Christ (see Rom. 8:17).

I am accepted by Christ (see Rom. 15:7).

I am the temple of the Holy Spirit (see 1 Cor. 6:19).

I am a new creature in Christ (see 2 Cor. 5:17).

I am set free in Christ (see Gal. 5:1).

I am chosen (see Eph. 1:4).

I am holy and blameless in His sight (see Eph. 1:4).

I am adopted into His family (see Eph. 1:5).

I am alive with Christ (see Eph. 2:4–5).

I am His masterpiece, His workmanship (see Eph. 2:10).

I am brought near to God and bought with a price (see Eph. 2:13).

I am cared for (see Phil. 4:19).

I am complete in Christ (see Col. 2:10).

This is just a short list of the descriptions God uses in reference to you. Just enough to pique your curiosity. (You will find a more extensive list in the appendix in the back of this book.) Take some time to study these verses. Then continue to delve into other verses that speak truth to your insecurities. Meditate on these truths. Dwell on them. Imagine giving God's opinions of you the same weight and credibility you've been giving all the other audiences in your life over the years. How incredibly transforming that could be. Imagine these truths trumping all the other experiences of your life. Trumping the conclusions you have previously made about yourself. Trumping the opinions others have of you. Allow God to speak these truths about your identity deep into the wells of your being. Take the time to dwell there in that place of freedom. Allow these truths to transform your mind, impacting how you think about yourself and healing your self-worth.

Do you notice the contrast between your first list of "I am" statements and the list God has given you? If you are like most of us, God's list looks a little (or a lot) different from the one you created. And these differences represent the gap where freedom is found.

His descriptors of you are your true identity. Say goodbye to your false identity. God, your Audience of One, rescues you with His truth. And this is who He says you are. This is who you are in sickness, and in health, for richer or poorer. In success and failure. When others accept you, and when they don't. When life is easy, and when you don't feel like you get a break. When you're having a good hair day, or when you've lost all your hair due to chemo.

These are solid, unshakable facts about you that cannot be swayed by temporary circumstance—good or bad. This is your *identity!* No more dizzying audiences. No more thieves. You can have freedom via a single audience.

AO1

Carson Wentz, quarterback for the Philadelphia Eagles, has a large audience. Wentz, the second overall pick of the 2016 NFL draft, is a household name among football enthusiasts. He has captured the attention of millions. And yet he has coined a phrase about the only audience that matters: AO1, short for "Audience of One."[1] He has AO1 inscribed on his cleats and tattooed on his wrist. A man with an audience of millions considers AO1 his life motto.

Why? He bases his motto on Romans 5:8, "God demonstrates His own love for us in this: While we were still sinners, Christ died for us." Despite his massive audience, Carson desires to live life with his focus on God as his audience, whether on or off the field. That's the kind of motto that will provide Carson stability through the ups and downs of his football career, the successes or failures of his physical performance, and the controversies that will come and go. Stability and security will be his as he genuinely follows this motto of AO1.

Carson gets it. He realizes that all our efforts to gain the acceptance of others are not impressive to God. We have to choose our audience.

But Isn't All the World a Stage?

But what if others *are* watching? What if I feel like I *have* to perform?

Yes, someone is always watching. But sometimes they aren't watching nearly as closely as you might think.

But can you imagine a life lived to impress God? With Him as your sole focus? Your life is a stage and only one Person is in the audience. You are free from the quest to impress anyone else. That is freedom.

I'm reminded of numerous times over the years when I've worked with a professional musician or someone who is heavily involved in leading church-related musical worship. They really are on a stage. Others really are watching. Occasionally, someone with this gift will also experience a season of crippling stage-related anxiety. When this happens, our discussion quickly shifts to the necessity of an Audience of One. A worship leader's task is simply to worship. When that leader allows his worship of God to be his sole focus, he permits everyone else in the room to figuratively fade into the background. This is when God takes the stage, and anxieties fall away. There is no posed performance, which removes the leader's fear of failure or need for admiration from onlookers. This shifting of focus to God alone is a salve for the performance- and approval-driven anxiety the worship leader is facing.

Life lived for an Audience of One is much the same. It is seeing life as an opportunity for worship. You'll never receive enough glory from the world's stage for you to feel innately significant. Instead, seek to impress God, and let the resulting light shine on the world so that others will see your goodness and lift God up (see Matt. 5:16). Let God take the stage. Incredible freedom is found there.

Brokenness Calls for Healing

If you are broken, you need a healing Savior. If you are a slave to a thief, you need a safe and protecting Lord. You need a friend who loves you at all times. He is your Audience of One. I've seen Him heal a broken identity more times than I could count. Yours is next. Trust Him. Yes, put all your eggs in His basket. He is trustworthy. AO1.

FREEDOM Q & A

1. You've been challenged in this chapter to consider living for an Audience of One. What is your reaction to this challenge? What are your concerns?

2. The many characteristics of God include: stable, wise, safe, protective, merciful, relational, sovereign. He exhibits each of these characteristics to perfection and completeness. How does this make you feel about Him being your Audience of One? Can you depend on Him for your identity? Be honest with Him—and with yourself. Consider any fears about this idea of putting all your eggs in one basket. If you have fears about this, how do you plan to address them?

3. If you are going to trust in God as your Audience of One, it is important to discern how He defines you. Who does He say that you are? What is your response to His opinion of you? Remember, submission to God just means agreement. Can you agree with Him regarding your worth?

4. Yes, all the world might be a stage, but you don't have to live for that audience. You can live for a single audience member. How might this perspective inspire you to be an even more effective light to others? How might it free you?

14

Formula
for Wholeness

Why do we wrestle with self-worth? Because we each yearn to know that there is a reason for our existence. That we're not just on this earth to take up space. That there is something significant about us that explains and defines our presence in this thing called life.

But is freedom from insecurity really as simple as a formula? Yes . . . and no. You see, *freedom* and *wholeness* are relative words. You and I won't experience wholeness in its most complete form this side of eternity. We won't experience security in the most powerfully freeing manner until we are in the presence of our Maker. But can we experience it more fully? Is there space for freedom? You bet there is. And we needn't settle for anything less than the maximum amount of freedom possible on earth.

The formula for wholeness is more like building blocks than it is a formula.

Submission of Thoughts

Leads to

Stability of Emotions

Leads to

Purpose in Action

Culminating in

Freedom from Insecurity

Why building blocks? Because the formula won't work unless it starts with submission of thoughts. The formula cannot be rearranged.

Let's talk about each aspect of this formula and how together they culminate in the freedom we are seeking.

Submission of Thoughts

Insecurities rob us of psychological freedom, and negative ruminations are characteristic of a false identity. We've talked about some of the truths that characterize your true worth. But talking about truth and submitting to truth are two very different things. If you are desperate for freedom from your insecurity, then it's time to have an honest conversation about submitting your thoughts to God.

It might seem unfair of me to suggest this, since sometimes our finite minds conclude that we are nothing more than puppets with little control over our lives or our surroundings. At least we can control what we think about ourselves, right?

No. Not if we want to be whole.

You see, I am God's. And if you are my sister in Christ, you are also His. Therefore, as His possessions, we don't have the right to choose our thoughts. You heard me. *You don't have the right to choose your thoughts.* Nope. Not even your thoughts about yourself. And by submitting that tiny and personal shred of control you thought you had in this life, you will ultimately find freedom.

How?

Maybe you can see the value of submitting your thoughts to God. But how? Isn't that one of those things that sounds easier than it really is? Let's talk a little more specifically about what it means to submit our thoughts to God and how to do that.

What Am I to Think?

The first step of submitting our thoughts to God is to determine what to think. Let's look to the Word for instruction: "Finally, brothers and sisters, whatever is true, whatever is noble, whatever is right, whatever is pure, whatever is lovely, whatever is admirable—if anything is excellent or praiseworthy—think about such things" (Phil. 4:8). Nothing on this list is negative, insulting, or self-loathing. God wants such destructiveness out of our minds and our mouths. To achieve the mode of thinking described in Philippians 4, we are to depend on God to "guard" our hearts and minds (v. 7).

This Scripture doesn't suggest that we should *consider* thinking about these things. It matter-of-factly *commands* that we do them. We have no choice. If you and I want to have freedom from insecurities, then we *must* think in the manner God commands us to think. We *must* align our thoughts with Him.

Let's be more specific. Below is the beginning of Paul's letter to the church of Ephesus. The same truths that applied to them then apply to us today. These truths are the shapings of a true and healthy self-worth:

Praise be to the God and Father of our Lord Jesus Christ, who has blessed us in the heavenly realms with every spiritual blessing in Christ. For he chose us in him before the creation of the world to be holy and blameless in his sight. In love he predestined us for adoption to sonship through Jesus Christ, in accordance with his pleasure and will—to the praise of his glorious grace, which he has freely given us in the One he loves. In him we have redemption through his blood, the forgiveness of sins, in accordance with the riches of God's grace that he lavished on us. With all wisdom and understanding, he made known to us the mystery of his will according to his good pleasure, which he purposed in Christ, to be put into effect when the times reach their fulfillment—to bring unity to all things in heaven and on earth under Christ.

In him we were also chosen, having been predestined according to the plan of him who works out everything in conformity with the purpose of his will, in order that we, who were the first to put our hope in Christ, might be for the praise of his glory. And you also were included in Christ when you heard the message of truth, the gospel of your salvation. When you believed, you were marked in him with a seal, the promised Holy Spirit, who is a deposit guaranteeing our inheritance until the redemption of those who are God's possession—to the praise of his glory. (Eph. 1:3–14)

Review these verses once more, this time looking for adjectives that characterize you as God's child. Use a highlighter to mark the adjectives He uses to describe you. Then write them out in a list in the margin of this book. You probably listed *blessed, chosen, adopted, loved, redeemed, forgiven, included in Christ,* and *marked in him with a seal.*

Now consider all the verbs in that same section of Scripture. Highlight the verbs, and then also write them in the margin. Note that the adjectives are descriptors of you, and the verbs represent God's actions. These aren't just basic truths; they are action-oriented truths, revealing that God goes the extra measure in His love for and pursuit of you. Do you see it? Your worth is directly linked to His actions. *Your worth is not about your performance; it is about Him.* Who He is. What He's done. Therefore, your acceptance of Him, and His truth about you, frees you to become whole.

Now think on these things. Repent from any thought about yourself that is inconsistent with who God says you are. Yes, repent. Turn away. Reject. *Submit your thoughts to God.*

Persistence

Thinking once on these things can deliver a temporary, fresh perspective. But you won't experience anything transformational without *persistence*. You must think on them consistently, with repetition and meditation. Thinking on truth requires the same level of attention and dedication that years of thinking destructively required. Your destructive thoughts didn't just happen. You fertilized and nurtured them. You gave them your time and attention. You pondered them frequently and with deep concern. They were born out of persistence, with repetition and meditation. So cast your attention on God's truth, and dig in your heels. Stay there, pondering. Treasure the truth about yourself. Fertilize that truth. Nurture it through meditation and repetition. You get out of a destructive thought pattern the same way you got in: persistence. Learning by repetition makes information stick. This is why you still might be able to ride a bike, even if you haven't gotten on one in twenty years, or sing the lyrics of a song you haven't heard in decades. You rode a bike so many times that you'll never forget how to, and you heard that song so often that you'll never forget the lyrics.

Mimi

Let me demonstrate the power of repetition with a personal story. After a years-long battle with severe dementia, my grandmother (Mimi) couldn't tell me much about what was going on around her. She didn't know whether she had just eaten a meal, or what year it was. She couldn't remember my name, or even how she might know me. But in the hours prior to her death, when I asked if there was anything I could read to her that would bring her comfort, she immediately responded, "Psalm 23." And then I watched as her lips became evidence of her reciting this Scripture by memory as I read it aloud to her. Her repeating of Psalm 23 throughout her life had exceeded her dementia, which at that point had robbed her of almost everything. Because she had meditated on that psalm for years, it was still accessible to her in her time of need, despite her circumstances. If it's possible that repetition and meditation are more powerful than dementia, then we need to pay attention. This brings great hope that it can also be a formidable tool for overpowering insecurity.

Resist Satan

Submitting our thoughts to God is both offensive and defensive. And just like any good basketball game, offensive efforts won't win the game without some good defense to back them up. Determining our thoughts and being persistent in repeating and meditating on God's truth is our offensive strategy. But we must also defend ourselves against our enemy. Why? Because he wants to capture our minds, and he works diligently to twist the truth. He detests God and detests when we submit our thoughts to His truth.

Satan can't possess us, as we are children of God. But he can influence us. His ability to influence is based on his access. If we leave open even the slightest gap, then he takes that as an invitation. So we must guard aggressively. We must defensively resist him. "Resist the devil, and he will flee from you" (James 4:7).

Satan is an aggressor. And we are not in a ball game. Our struggle with him is a war, a spiritual war that requires spiritual strategies and weapons. Whenever I face a battle with the enemy,

I always turn to Ephesians 6:10–20. This chapter describes how we can prepare for an effective battle. It explains our offensive and defensive weapons. Since the moment we were saved, we have all had access to the armor described in Ephesians 6. We just have to put it on. Deliberately and intentionally. Every day we have truth through the Word of God, we have the righteousness of Christ, and we have the shoes of peace.

We also have the helmet of salvation.

This is a spiritual helmet—because we are in a spiritual war. This spiritual helmet offers us important protection, because if the enemy can get to our minds and thoughts, he can get to our emotions and actions as well.

The helmet of salvation doesn't provide our salvation; rather, it is the confidence of our salvation and the reassurance that we belong to God. It is a reflection on an eternal perspective, God's promises to us, and our future battle victory. Our helmet is a visual representation of a perspective of truth. With the helmet of salvation fitted over our minds, we can easily visualize a destructive thought coming toward us and then bouncing away. Just as a physical helmet, such as a bike or football helmet, prevents a pebble from hitting our skulls, this perspective can prevent a negative thought from penetrating our minds. Our helmets provide protection against Satan, who accuses, exaggerates, tempts, and causes doubt. And with access to the Word of God, we can overcome Satan. God's Word is our sword, a sword that stops Satan in his tracks. And we can stand on that truth.

Submit to God

Submitting our thoughts to God also requires us to *submit to God*. "Jesus said, 'If you hold to my teaching, you are really my disciples. Then you will know the truth, and the truth will set you free'" (John 8:31–32). Freedom is what we are after—and submission to God is the bridge. We must stay close to Him, abiding with Him and surrendering to His commands. When we submit and live life with Him, He transforms the old to the new. "Therefore, if anyone is in Christ, the new creation has come: The old has gone, the new is here!" (2 Cor. 5:17). When we submit to God, our old thinking begins to die out. Our old, broken identity is released, and a new one is born.

One of my favorite Scriptures is found in Isaiah. "Forget the former things; do not dwell on the past. See, I am doing a new thing! Now it springs up; do you not perceive it? I am making a way in the wilderness and streams in the wasteland" (Isa. 43:18–19). Submitting to God means forgetting who you think you are. Forget your failures—and your successes. Forget the insults—and the accolades. Forget the experiences—good and bad. Forget your roles, your jobs, your diplomas. Forget your skin color and your bank account. Forget your relationships or the absence of them. Submitting to God means you start with a clean canvas and allow Him to hold the brush. Let Him paint the new picture of who you are. This is not selective amnesia. Rather, it is simply welcoming a clean slate. There's no scarlet letter. If you have been struggling, then it's time for an about-face. Turn your attention in the opposite direction—toward truth, toward your new identity—from this point forward.

Submitting to God means agreeing with Him. Agreeing with Him about your identity. Agreeing with Him about your thoughts. Put away your old thinking. Turn away from who you may have thought you were. If you've struggled with self-worth, then your old self-image has simply been wrong. Once you've agreed with Him, you will be positioned for a powerful transformation toward wholeness. Then you can prepare to experience the refreshing that comes from wholeness. Your new thoughts are not toxic thoughts, like the ones that might have dominated your mind previously. These are not focused on the past. They aren't based on comparisons. You don't have tunnel vision. These thoughts are healthy and eternally focused. And there's more. These thoughts deliver stable, healthy emotions.

Stability of Emotions

The good news is that stable emotions are a passive by-product of healthy thoughts. All the work that goes into changing the way you think pays off. You don't really have to work at stabilizing your emotions as long as you've done the hard work of stabilizing your thoughts. So enjoy the rewards of stability. You're off the roller coaster! Your emotions no longer have to be unpredictable or overpowering, vacillating rapidly with each slight change of circumstance. You no longer have to be controlled by overwhelming negative emotions. Notice that the word *stable* is a carefully chosen one. If we were in a hospital listed in stable condition, we would not be considered perfectly cured. The same is true for our emotions. Our emotions will challenge us from time to time. But when we struggle with insecurities, our emotions could be considered in critical condition. Our journey to wholeness, and the stabilizing of our thoughts, takes our emotional well-being from critical to stable. I don't know about you, but I'll take stable over critical any day.

Purpose in Action

Actions are a by-product of our thoughts and emotions. We can probably all agree that secure people act differently from insecure people. I'm sure you know the phrase "Actions speak louder than words."

Consider Paul's reminder to the church of Ephesus: "For we are God's handiwork, created in Christ Jesus to do good works, which God prepared in advance for us to do" (Eph. 2:10). Our works are our actions, and we were created to complete God-honoring actions. But often we don't have the confidence to pursue God's calling. We forget the first part of the verse, that we are "God's handiwork." Our actions (our works) reflect our beliefs about ourselves. Without a healthy and accurate self-worth, we are slaves to a false identity. We can't be freed to be the royalty we really are. Consider the timidity that comes with slavery versus the boldness that comes with royalty. That's a picture of how our self-worth, true or false, impacts our actions.

The actions of a truly secure person are fueled by purpose, without the agenda of a search for approval. With their thoughts focused on truth and their emotions steadied, a secure person is positioned to participate with God for His purpose. A secure person partners with God and pours themselves into the lives of others. They don't exhaust or tear others down (they are without drama); instead, they seek to build others up in a way that brings value to their lives. The eternal perspective of a secure person allows them to grasp their purpose. They embrace the significance of their creation and individuality, of their strengths and gifts. They embrace their purpose. And they act on it. An added benefit? They become even more secure as they experience God using them for His purpose. It is a beautiful picture of self-worth lived out how God intended.

Freedom from Insecurity

Submitting our thoughts stabilizes our emotions and brings purpose to our actions. This is the formula for wholeness. But what does wholeness look like on a practical level in the lives of real people? We're going to spend the remainder of this book exploring how this formula will transform your life, and we're going to meet some people whose freedom has resulted in a life of boldness and purpose. If you are on this journey, then I hope you will find their freedom to be inspiring and contagious.

VICTORY VERSE

"For we are God's handiwork, created in Christ Jesus to do good works, which God prepared in advance for us to do."

EPHESIANS 2:10

1. How might application of the formula for wholeness (Submission of Thoughts, *leading to* Stability of Emotions, *leading to* Purpose in Action) impact your life?

2. What progress are you making in submitting your thoughts to God?

3. What progress have you made regarding the stability of your emotions?

4. How is this progress impacting your actions? Your responses to situations?

5. How is God healing your identity?

15

A Transformation
in Dependence

We spent a lot of time in the last chapter focusing on a formula for wholeness. Let me be clear: going through the motions and following this step-by-step formula superficially will not provide freedom. It is the submission to God (a necessary ingredient of the first step of this formula) that transforms our healing from superficial to genuine. From a false sense of freedom to authentic and indisputable freedom. No longer are we dependent on earthly measures of worth. And when that dependence begins to shift, everything else in our lives also shifts.

What does this transformation in dependence look like? The easiest way to draw a picture of this transformation is to consider its characteristics.

Acceptance of Weaknesses—and Strengths

Wholeness allows us to see our inadequacies for what they are. Nothing more. Nothing less. Wholeness allows us to also see our strengths for what they are. Nothing more. Nothing less. Wholeness allows us to take a matter-of-fact, objective, and accepting stance regarding ourselves.

Can we accept that we all have weaknesses? We all experience feelings of inadequacy. But these don't make us inadequate as a whole. Weakness is a characteristic we share as human beings, much like the fact that we share a normal body temperature of roughly 98.6 degrees.

Those who know me well know I am directionally deficient. My dad lovingly jokes that I have a hard time finding my way out of a U-turn. While I'm perhaps not quite that deficient, it is certainly a severe weak spot of mine, and one that requires deliberate dependence on GPS (thank God for smartphones). But my lack of a sense of direction doesn't define me. It's just one of my quirks. And we all have quirks.

Can we also accept that we all have strengths? Areas in which we contribute something valuable to the body of Christ. Yes, you are significant. You have God-created strengths. Wholeness will allow you to humbly acknowledge and appreciate those strengths.

Each of us is assigned spiritual gifts at the time of our salvation. Accepting these strengths is crucial for us in assuming God's purpose for our lives. This doesn't mean we are arrogant about our strengths. It simply means we accept them and allow God to use and further develop them in our lives.

Absence of Comparisons

Can you imagine appreciating the value of a sister's strengths without feeling the compulsion to compare yourself to her? Without feeling threatened that you don't measure up? Of course you don't measure up. What you see is her strength, her gift. You have your gifts and strengths, and she has hers. One does not take away from the other. Wholeness frees you to celebrate when God uses her strengths to shine for Him. She's not the standard for comparison—God is.

Though your compulsion to compare yourself to others will come automatically, you can quickly shoo away such thoughts and refuse to be held captive by them. When the annoying pest of comparison comes your way, remind yourself that everyone has a story. Everyone has strengths and weaknesses, successes and failures, approvals and rejections. Allow yourself to embrace the rest of their story, and the comparison (the enemy) will flee. Truth is the cure. You see, everyone is the same at the foot of the cross. We all struggle with insecurities and are in desperate need of God's transforming power and help in our lives. So it's time for us to rise above the crippling comparisons that keep us chained.

Edification

Absent of comparisons, wholeness frees us to edify others. It opens up possibilities for us to encourage, build up, equip, and mentor others. Without being plagued by a false identity that fuels a self-focused concern that others may rise above you, you are free to experience the satisfaction of pouring into the lives of those around you, of taking others under your wing and offering wisdom and affirmation that will help them discover their own identity as well as allow them to be more effective in the body of Christ.

Beauty

Wholeness frees us to care for our bodies and our appearance, and to present ourselves with both an inner and outer beauty. This is not a quest for beauty that only drives more insecurities. Rather, it is an embracing of our physical self, just as God has made us, and a striving to be the best we can be. It means taking care of ourselves physically, strengthening our bodies with exercise and nutrition. It means showering and looking nice. Consider the woman described in Proverbs 31. She didn't present herself in a manner that expressed a lack of care. Instead, she was "clothed in fine linen and purple" (v. 22). And she took care of herself physically, as her arms were "strong for her tasks" (v. 17). Wholeness doesn't mean being reckless with our appearance because we are too confident to care. But it also doesn't mean having an obsession with appearance. It's a beautiful balance of the embracing of our physical selves. It's okay to work to be beautiful with the body God has given each of us. So, let's take pleasure in cultivating our beauty at the age that we are and working to be fit and physically strong for the tasks we face. A healthy approach to beauty is neither pretending it is unimportant nor making it an idol.

Boldness

Wholeness frees us from the hindrance of timidity and provides us a backbone. It invites an effective boldness for any occasion. Fearfulness is cast aside. Fear of failing or fear of rejection no longer influences our decisions. We can speak with confidence. We can ambitiously take risks that we feel God is leading us to take. We can set healthy boundaries or confront others when necessary. Wholeness provides boldness—that essential ingredient for accomplishing God's will in our lives.

Note that boldness doesn't necessarily mean "without anxiety." Those who have a predisposition to anxiety may still experience some anxious symptoms, but they do so with a boldness that prevents them from avoiding the things they fear. Boldness prevents their anxiousness from shrinking their world.

Humility

It might seem odd that humility would follow boldness. But these two characteristics are not mutually exclusive. Humility doesn't mean we loathe ourselves. It just means we are not preoccupied with ourselves. We can love the person God made us to be without being arrogant. And we can hate our fleshly and sinful nature without self-scorn. Humility means we simply have a sobering, realistic view of ourselves. "Do not think of yourself more highly than you ought, but rather think of yourself with sober judgment" (Rom. 12:3). Genuine humility is a beautiful fruit born of a healthy identity.

Teachable Spirit

Since security doesn't mean arrogance but does mean a godly and healthy humility, it is fitting that with a healthy self-worth, we also gain a teachable spirit. A healthy wholeness doesn't lead to being a know-it-all. It does mean, however, that we recognize our weak spots. And we recognize those strengths and gifts in others without being threatened by their expertise. A teachable spirit is a genuine eagerness to learn from the strengths of others and a desire to be sharpened and challenged by them.

Healthy Relationships

Wholeness invites relationships, and we were designed to be in re-lationships with others. But not just any kind of relationships. With healing, we no longer need to avoid others for fear of rejection. We no longer feel desperate for relationships. We no longer settle for destructive relationships. Wholeness allows us the freedom to live within meaningful relationships without codependency and without drama. When we have a healthy self-worth, we are free to edify and encourage others within our relationships, because doing so poses no threat to our worth.

Productive Emotions

Healing from insecurities doesn't mean we are without emotions. It doesn't even mean we are without negative emotions. It just means that our emotions are guided by objective truth and allowed to work purposefully rather than destructively. When we have our emotions stabilized, they can better fuel us to express healthy responses. Emotions aren't bad. For example, happiness can lead to laughter and bonding with a friend, improving our overall health. Fear can assist us in creating a safety plan. Anger can fuel within us an appropriate response to injustice. God created us with the capacity to feel—and to feel deeply. Insecurities rob us of stability and can leave us feeling as if we're going crazy. But freedom from insecurities prunes away the destructiveness and allows our emotions to work purposefully in their pure form.

Eternal Perspective

Wholeness transforms our tunnel vision into godly vision. When we're insecure, we get drawn into the circumstances before us. We can't see beyond ourselves because we are desperately seeking self-preservation. When our identity is transformed, the desperation subsides and we are freed to ponder beyond our immediate situation. We have space to consider eternity. An eternal perspective has a transforming power all on its own. A power that allows us to process the world differently. In one sense, this perspective is calming. ("In light of eternity, does my body weight really matter?") In another sense, this perspective creates urgency. ("Eternity is all that matters; I want to get busy purposefully devoting my life to things that will last forever and using my gifts while I can.") An eternal perspective is the only true perspective. And our freedom from the chains of insecurity allows us to live life more predominantly from that healthier perspective.

An Example

When I study Scripture in search of a person with these characteristics who has been transformed by wholeness, I am particularly moved by the life of Paul. Paul was a living demonstration of a transformation in dependence.

Based on his history, Paul would have had every reason to be insecure as a Christian. He easily could have carried shame for how he had previously persecuted Christians. He could have felt that he was unworthy and useless to God. He could have struggled with the judgment and rejection he experienced from the Christian community following his conversion. But because Paul accepted the truth about his identity, he was radically transformed. Remember, Paul also had a name change (previously Saul). And because he accepted the truth about his identity, he was also able to call himself by his new name.

We can learn from Paul. Over and over again in Scripture, we see Paul humbly but boldly, matter-of-factly, and unapologetically speak truth and point others to Christ. He was able to speak with confidence. Sometimes his words were strongly challenging, prophesying the demise of the person in front of him. Sometimes his words were full of thankfulness and appreciation. Other times he spoke boldly about the gospel and what he knew Jesus had done. He didn't alter his words to get approval. He spoke the truth for the occasion. Oftentimes, Paul was the "chief speaker" among his friends. And he spoke not with timidity but with effectiveness (see Acts 14). He was an encourager and worked to build up and edify the church. One must be confident in themselves to have the ability to affirm others.

Paul had a healthy boldness that comes only from a secure identity. In the face of judgment or rejection, a person with a fragile sense of self cowers to the pressure for approval. But a secure person stands with a backbone, speaks the truth, and ultimately changes the world—one interaction at a time. No drama. No swaying of emotion. Wholeness brings a steadiness and certainty that fuels purpose. And Paul was certainly a purpose chaser.

Paul's name meant "little," but he never let his name define him. Though Paul clearly thought little of his needs, he thought much of God and accepted who God defined him as being. He was not an arrogant person, but he did not hesitate to boast loudly about God. Instead of being little, Paul lived powerfully and became one of the most influential and persuasive individuals in history.

One of the apparent keys to Paul's identity, stability, and effectiveness was his resistance to isolation. Paul was separated from people only when he was jailed for his faith. And upon his release, he wasted no time finding fellowship with believers. He was constantly surrounded by companions and made maintaining his relationships a top priority. In fact, he experienced great inconveniences because he chose to check on friends and encourage others face-to-face or by letter. But Paul was not codependent. He didn't find his worth in those relationships. He found his worth in Christ and was so full of that assurance that he had an overflow to share with others. Wholeness allows for this kind of wonderfully healthy and inspiring relationship.

Yes, Paul chased purpose . . . and relationships. This combination of chasing is why Paul also had a heart for the next generation. An insecure person wants the focus to be on themselves and is hesitant to mentor others for fear that they will become greater. But not Paul. Paul generously encouraged and mentored others and is noted for taking Timothy under his wing. Paul allowed God to use him to shape Timothy's ministry and further spread the gospel. The most effective leaders are those who prepare their successors. And only a leader with a healthy identity can make plans for successorship.

I recently saw the movie *Cars 3* with my family. The movie's underlying theme is personal identity. We discover the vulnerabilities that cause Lightning McQueen as well as his trainer, Cruz, to struggle with their identities. And we see the limitations that a false worth creates. Lightning McQueen discovers at the end of the movie that his greatest satisfaction is in helping someone else along. As he edifies Cruz, he helps her discover that she wasn't born to be a trainer. She was born to be a racer. He speaks truth into her life in a manner that frees her from the past messages that have trapped and limited her. And in doing so, Lightning McQueen experiences great purpose and fulfillment. Lightning McQueen isn't real. But the message of the movie is a real message—one that Paul also discovered as he experienced the satisfaction of mentoring Timothy. His encouragement of others was an encouragement to himself. Because he was not limited by a false identity, he was free to experience the rush of edifying others and helping them discover their true identity. Paul was a light.

Bioluminescence

About a month ago, I received the disappointing email that I had lost the lottery for the blue ghost fireflies tour in the DuPont Forest in North Carolina. I had so looked forward to this outing for my family. You see, for just a few short weeks, the fireflies cause the DuPont Forest floor to be covered by gorgeous blue light. These blue fireflies have brought such fascination and so many people that a lottery had to be instituted to limit the number of guests. Why? Because the females can't fly, and many of them were being squashed on the forest floor as guests trampled off the trails to get a closer look. There is something about a light in the darkness that draws us to it. We just can't get enough. And these blue fireflies are a beautiful example of that truth.

Now to the word—*bioluminescence*. What in the world does that mean? It is simply the emission of light by an organism. Blue fireflies are *living light*.

Paul was a living light because he was free to live purposefully without the shackles of a broken self-worth. I too want to be a living light. You probably do as well.

To be a living light is the crux of our God-designed identity. "You will shine among them like stars in the sky" (Phil. 2:15). He created us for bioluminescence! "You are the light of the world.

A town built on a hill cannot be hidden. Neither do people light a lamp and put it under a bowl. Instead they put it on its stand, and it gives light to everyone in the house. In the same way, let your light shine before others, that they may see your good deeds and glorify your Father in heaven" (Matt. 5:14–16).

So, shine brightly, my friend. Your light will be a fascinating and encouraging sight to behold to others in a forest of darkness. You are bioluminescence. Free from the grip of insecurities, you are designed to shine. Let wholeness transform your insecurities into *living light*.

VICTORY VERSE

"You will shine among them like stars in the sky."

PHILIPPIANS 2:15

FREEDOM Q & A

1. Consider the list of characteristics that reflect a transformation in dependence from worldly measures of worth to a healthy identity. Which characteristics are the most endearing to you? Which ones do you most want to see in your life?

2. As you begin this healing journey, which characteristics do you already see God developing in you?

3. Consider Paul's history. How does the contrast of his old versus new identity encourage you? How is God using Paul's example to speak truth into your life?

16

Freedom from Insecurity— A Biblical Example

When we think of being secure in ourselves, we often think of being empowered. Walking tall and strong with our head held high and our nose in the air. Confidence means building ourselves up with pep talks and preparing to battle life aggressively, right? But that kind of empowering has never freed anyone from insecurities. In fact, it often comes across as being arrogant. Our society has sent us so many confusing messages about what it means to be secure.

We need another example of wholeness. We need a mentor. Someone who lived a full life. Someone who lived with heartaches and struggles, just like you and I do. Someone who experienced successes, just like you and I do. Someone who lived the highs and the lows of life. Someone who lived with a healthy identity and was not swayed by their failures or their successes. A female with freedom and wholeness, whose security didn't depend on her circumstances.

Meet Esther. When we hear Esther's name, we automatically think of *Queen* Esther. We think, *Sure, she had a healthy self-worth—she was a queen!* But Esther's life wasn't as easy as it might appear to have been at first glance. In fact, if ever there was a woman who experienced trauma and pain, it was Esther. And if ever there was a woman who was whole—despite trauma and tragedy, royalty and infamy—it was Esther. Was she perfect? No. She was human, just like you and I are. But was she free from insecurity? It certainly seems so. How did she get there? And what did wholeness look like in her life? Let's take a look.

To get the full effect, I suggest you read Esther's story in the Old Testament book by the same name. Hers is a story meant for the big screen, so you will certainly enjoy your time there. I'm going to summarize her story here, but you'll miss some interesting details if you skip reading it yourself.

We are first introduced to Esther as Hadassah in the second chapter of the book of Esther. She is identified as a young Jewish girl living in the citadel of Susa, and whose mother and father had both died. While we don't know the specifics of their deaths, we do know she lost both her parents and was orphaned. The Bible says she was taken in by her cousin Mordecai, who raised her as his own child and loved her immensely. We also learn she was taken into captivity as a very young girl, along with many other Jews. By definition, the word *captivity* suggests force. She wasn't offered a choice. Her early years were tragic and difficult. Esther knew emotional pain, and the circumstances of her youth certainly would have left her vulnerable to insecurities.

Esther grew up during the reign of King Xerxes. His beautiful queen, Vashti, was probably a common name to Esther. To a little girl growing up in Susa, the queen was probably to Esther like a young movie star is to today's young girls. The queen was a beautiful woman who had everything a woman could possibly want (or so it probably appeared to any young girl who watched from the outside).

After refusing to respond to a request to appear before the arrogant King Xerxes, Queen Vashti was hastily removed from her royal position. This vacancy led to the most flamboyant, and twisted, beauty pageant in all of history. The search began for beautiful, young virgin girls. Girls from every one of the 127 provinces were chosen and brought to the king. "Esther was also taken" (2:8). *Taken*. Again. This was not a beauty pageant that young girls signed up for. Esther was kidnapped. This time she was held captive in the king's harem. This was sex trafficking ordered by the king himself.

Esther had already encountered many circumstances that could have threatened her identity. And here was another. Esther's only options were to be broken and traumatized by another captivity or become as resilient as possible in the most extraordinary experience of her life.

Can you imagine being in the king's harem? Talk about drama. It was a massive effort, involving hundreds and hundreds of officials and workers in this quest for the next queen. Esther 2:12–14 describes the journey to the palace:

> Before a young woman's turn came to go in to King Xerxes, she had to complete twelve months of beauty treatments prescribed for the women, six months with oil of myrrh and six with perfumes and cosmetics. And this is how she would go to the king: Anything she wanted was given her to take with her from the harem to the king's palace. In the evening she would go there and in the morning return to another part of the harem to the care of Shaashgaz, the king's eunuch who was in charge of the concubines. She would not return to the king unless he was pleased with her and summoned her by name.

Think about this. It was like a solid year of having maids at your disposal, with ongoing access to the best salons, clothing, jewelry, massage therapists, restaurants, and fitness coaches. Sounds like a dream, doesn't it? In all reality, it was a dark, twisted, competitive, and *involuntary* beauty pageant. For all but one, the twelve months of preparation ended with a solitary night with the king and permanent assignment to another part of the harem.

In the midst of this dark drama stood Esther. She undoubtedly was chosen to move into the king's harem because of her striking beauty. But once there, it was both her inner and outer beauty that won the favor of Hegai, one of the king's eunuchs. Her inner beauty, her humble security in herself, made her shine among the crowd.

When I imagine Esther in this situation, I wonder if she mentored other girls in the harem in the same way that Mordecai had mentored her. Perhaps she spoke the same truths to them that Mordecai had spoken to her, assuring them of their true identity despite their circumstances. Perhaps she comforted them when they were grieving being away from their families, for she would have been well-acquainted with grief. I can imagine Esther complimenting and affirming the other girls regarding their beauty and their strengths. I don't know exactly how Esther interacted with these other girls, but something obviously radiated from within her, causing everyone around her to feel comfortable with her. As a result of this favor, Hegai pampered Esther with special treatments, apparently even sweeter than what the other ladies experienced. My goodness, she had seven maids all to herself and the best suite in the harem. She went from being a young orphan girl to prize of the king's harem, receiving all the treatment of royalty. This was more dramatic than a modern-day reality TV show!

As the months passed by, Esther likely made the best of her situation. Perhaps she even enjoyed some of the luxuries that royalty offered, but she never forgot where she came from. I think she remained humbled by her beginnings but certainly not broken by her past. She remained grounded by Mordecai's influence and clearly never ceased to be teachable. According to Esther 2:15, when the time came for Esther to go to the king, she asked for nothing other than what Hegai had suggested. Esther could have taken *anything* with her from the harem to the king's palace. Hegai recommended some things, but it doesn't appear that he was extravagant in his recommendation. Just imagine the fancy, lush materials and vibrant colors available to her, the priciest of perfumes, and the expanse of cosmetics. I bet lace and velvet ran amuck in the harem. Yet Esther denied herself some of those luxuries at the advice of someone who had her best interests in mind. Only when someone is grounded and secure can they deny themselves the indulgences that are at their fingertips.

Esther was just as teachable in the midst of royal captivity as she was when she was in orphaned captivity. She was willing to be instructed. Esther knew whom she could trust, and when those people advised her, she listened and submitted with a humble heart. This humility kept her grounded, living with wholeness and in reality, despite the jaw-dropping drama that enfolded her.

When Esther went to the king, she found his favor in the same way she had found the favor of so many others. King Xerxes chose Esther to be queen. Frankly, I think God had the king's heart in His hands. In an amazing twist of fate, Esther now wore the crown of the one she probably fantasized being as a young girl playing dress up. She moved into the palace with all its royal privileges. The king threw a banquet and even named a holiday in Esther's honor. Let the festivities and the fairy tale begin!

But it was no fairy tale. Yes, Esther was selected as queen. And that might seem like the greatest thing ever. But this king was a jerk with an anger issue, probably an alcohol problem, and not a bit of respect for women. Esther was captive once again—this time as an inmate of the royal palace.

But Esther's story doesn't end here. There was more drama to come. And the challenges to Esther's identity were far from over.

After she was named queen and all the festivities subsided, the Bible says she continued to honor Mordecai's instructions to keep her Jewish ancestry a secret, just as she had always done growing up (see Esther 2:10, 20). Esther also continued to find ways to communicate with her cousin. Mordecai guarded one of the palace gates, so he was always in close proximity. Esther didn't allow royal life to get to her, even though she was probably becoming more and more accustomed to the life of exclusive luxury with each passing day. She remained grounded in reality and kept her faithful promise to her cousin. Esther's genuine wholeness, which was unaltered by her tough circumstances, kept this royal queen humble enough to faithfully honor the advice of her gatekeeper cousin.

God placed Esther in this royal position because He had a task for her to accomplish; God was using her "for such a time as this" (4:14). She soon discovered that Haman, the king's right-hand man, had plans to annihilate the entire Jewish nation.

Had Esther gotten too attached to her new lifestyle in the palace with the arrogant king, she would have turned a blind eye to the hardships of her people. Instead, she was about to earn even greater respect from the king as she boldly lived in the truth and began another brave and intense journey—this one taking her from royalty to hero.

Esther fasted for three days. Given what we know of her past, this trial was probably not the first one that had led her to fast. Despite her position of royalty, despite now being a household name, Esther clearly depended on an Audience of One. This is grand evidence of her wholeness. After those three days of fasting, Esther began to put her plan to save her people into motion. She had to appeal to the king. She dressed in her very best robes and took the risk of appearing uninvited before the king—a move that could have cost Esther her life. Can you imagine the thoughts that were swirling through her head as she approached the inner court? She must have been a nervous wreck. I'm sure Hegai and all Esther's maids were also consumed with anxiety. Esther would have been keenly aware that the clothes she wore could have just as easily been her royal burial clothes. But she remained grounded and realistic, counting her steps into the inner court as though they could be her very last.

But Esther had been coached by Hegai years before, and she continued to respect his instruction. As a result, she knew precisely how to present herself to make the best impression on the king, and she did just that. Immediately upon seeing her, Xerxes extended the scepter and invited her to speak. Ah! Sigh of relief. She had survived the uninvited appearance and now had to move on to the next portion of her royal plan.

Esther knew her king well, and she knew how to influence him. She had just fasted for three days because she was aware that the odds were against her. First, she had to reveal to the king that she was a Jew. Then she had to tell him that his right-hand man was an evil liar, and the man who had once saved his life was also her Jewish cousin and adoptive father. And she also had to beg the king to spare the lives of her people. Keep in mind, as a result of Haman's manipulative and evil plan, the king had already sealed an *irreversible* order to exterminate the entire Jewish nation. And Esther was well aware of this fatal decree. Thank goodness Esther didn't have unrealistic expectations about her task ahead. Thank goodness she didn't have a false self-worth that would have stolen her voice and starved her boldness. Had she, she would have run away from the task in front of her. Thank goodness she didn't have a false self-worth that led to arrogance and entitlement. Had she, she would have taken a careless approach that would have led to evil Haman's immediate victory and the massacre of her people.

Instead, Esther calculated a magnificent, humble plan involving her beauty, her service, some alcohol, invitations to good ol' Haman to attend a banquet, and the best foods—all favorites of the king. I don't know how she persevered through all the bragging that must have taken place with those two difficult men both at the table during the banquet. But obviously she left them both curious to know her ultimate request. Because Esther knew what it would require to safely expose the truth to the king, she arranged for a second banquet.

Esther's timing showed patience and precision. Her efforts obviously impressed the king; he probably loved the mysteriousness of his queen calling such attention to himself. He was so taken with her that several times prior to her final spoken request, he promised her up to half of the kingdom. Insecurities would have caused her to jump hastily at his first offer, but Esther was too grounded for a knee-jerk reaction. She knew her king. And she knew Haman. She didn't look at her reality through rose-colored glasses. She knew it would require perfect timing and preparation to save her people. And she brilliantly served her way through two risky banquets until it was time to make the final eloquent presentation of her earnest request.

The result? The rise of her people, and the fall of Haman. Not only was Mordecai's life spared, but he was placed second in rank to King Xerxes and given authority over Haman's estate.

How did all this happen? It was because God used an unsuspecting, traumatized young girl with a resilient identity and placed her in a dark world of royalty. How did Esther respond to this life of royalty? Esther clearly lived "in" that world but not "of" it. Yes, she lived in that twisted royal world, but it did not live in her. Let's consider some other characteristics that surrounded Esther's healthy identity.

Esther's Characteristics of Wholeness

Esther was a picture of wholeness. She radiated all the characteristics of wholeness we discussed in the last chapter. Esther embraced her beauty and cared for her body and her appearance, but she also accepted her weaknesses and strengths. She didn't seem to be influenced by comparisons, and she was free to edify others. She lived a beautiful balance of boldness and humility, and she had a teachable spirit. She had healthy relationships and productive emotions. And because she lived with an eternal perspective, she was also a living light.

Esther was whole, which meant she wasn't codependent. She didn't need to be needed. She didn't have to have the attention of the king. Even in a royal world, she never expected of Xerxes what she knew he was incapable of providing as a mate. She lived as a queen in a fairy-tale palace, but she knew her selfish, perverse king was anyone but prince charming. She made the very most of the reality in which she found herself. She wasn't a complainer or a critic. She didn't appear to create drama or act on her emotions. She appeared to be emotionally stable. She kept her head on straight, her expectations tamed, and her goals truth-focused. She didn't deny or minimize her real challenges but instead addressed them bravely, wisely, and responsibly. She didn't have a false identity that was caught up in her royal life. On the contrary, *she was willing to lose her royal identity, and even her life, to be true to her real identity.* We see no hint of her being self-absorbed or self-serving, but instead, she was respectful, conscientious, and courteous. Lastly, as difficult a man as Xerxes probably was, Esther never gave up on his potential. She gave him opportunities to save face and to make wise decisions, and she probably allowed him to succeed in his relationship with her to the fullest extent his flesh was capable of. She didn't put out a halfhearted effort. Esther knew her reality required so much more of her. I'm thankful she had a secure identity. God used this security to provide her with the resilience she needed to bounce back from the enormous obstacles and challenges of her life. And by studying Esther, we can learn to do the same.

Esther's Inner Beauty

The Scriptures say Esther "won the favor of everyone who saw her" (Esther 2:15). But how? Esther's outer beauty goes without saying. But beautiful young girls were everywhere. She was just one of many gorgeous young women. What made Esther stand out in a crowd? Her inner beauty radiated, showing something was unique about her. And much more than just a healthy self-confidence made her shine.

The best way to summarize Esther's inner beauty is what the New Testament refers to in Galatians 5:22–23 as the fruit of the Spirit: "Love, joy, peace, forbearance, kindness, goodness, faithfulness, gentleness and self-control." Esther radiated because God shined through her. Hers was a genuine beauty that others found irresistible. Esther was a living example of true beauty from the inside out.

So, if you and I want radiating beauty, it will likewise be through the evidence of the Holy Spirit living in us. Christ within us creates a captivating, genuine beauty that illuminates the living light we've discussed in earlier chapters. He is what shines and makes us even more beautiful. This is a beauty that doesn't fade with aging. It's a beauty that makes us stand out among a large number of gorgeous women. And it is a beauty that shines in the darkness.

A Reality Check

My dear sisters, if you feel that Esther is a world away, let me bring you back to reality. Esther experienced various circumstances during the different seasons of her life. She experienced enormous pain, traumas, and poverty. Experiences that could have broken her. She also faced enormous successes. She was surrounded by extreme worldly blessings and pampering. So many things were fighting to impact her identity. Good things. Bad things. Her life circumstances. Her background. Her undeniable physical beauty. Her traumas. Her privileges. Her relationships. But she protected her identity against these thieves. Her worth was not altered by her triumphs. Or her tragedies. She didn't allow her identity to be attached to anything temporary. She relied solely on her Audience of One. As a result, she was of sound mind and stable emotions. She was teachable, with a healthy humility. She was able to engage in healthy relationships and make the most of those that weren't healthy. She was able to bounce back from life's hurts and is a beautiful picture of resilience.

Esther is evidence that you don't need to have riches or to be royalty to have a healthy sense of significance, and you don't have to have experienced poverty and trauma to possess healthy humility. You are no different from Esther. You have faced pain and traumas. You have experienced successes. You have many things fighting for your identity. Good things. Bad things. Life experiences. Your background. Your physical appearance. Your relationships. And did you know that if you have trusted in Jesus as Savior and Lord, you too are royalty? According to 1 Peter 2:9, "But you are a chosen people, a royal priesthood, a holy nation, God's special possession, that you may declare the praises of him who called you out of darkness into his wonderful light."

This too is your reality. You also were created and saved "for such a time as this." Like Esther, won't you embrace your real identity? If you are God's child, you too are chosen. Royal. Holy. You belong to God. Won't you embrace your Audience of One, starving out your attachment to all the other voices in your life? Just like Esther, God has created you to live in freedom with Him. He's called you out of the darkness and into the light, free from the insecurities that have robbed you. Free to praise Him. It's time to release those shackles and embrace the real identity God has declared for you.

VICTORY VERSE

"And who knows but that you have come to your royal position for such a time as this?"

— ESTHER 4:14

1. How can you relate to Esther's successes and privileges? How do you think those privileges impacted Esther's identity?

2. What successes and privileges have you experienced? How have these impacted your identity?

3. How can you relate to some of the challenges and traumas Esther experienced? How do you think these impacted her identity?

4. How would you summarize your own challenges and traumas? How have those personal struggles impacted your identity?

5. How do you think Esther's self-worth was protected from the positive or negative impacts of her various life experiences?

6. Esther shined, even among a large number of beautiful young women. How do you think the fruit of the Spirit caused Esther to radiate?

7. Esther embraced her cousin's conclusion that she was appointed her royal position "for such a time as this." Can you relate? If so, how? Describe the circumstances that involved such assurance of purpose. How did that experience impact your personal identity?

Conclusion

It's time to relinquish your insecurities, my friend. God's truths can rescue you from the oppression of your false beliefs, but only if you allow it to happen. Only if you agree. Only if you submit your thoughts to His thoughts. Reading this book won't transform you, but it is based on a perfect Author and His perfectly authored book that *will* transform you.

Jesus never allowed others to define Him. He defined Himself. "Light of the world." "Son of Man." "I am." And He did this defining with assertiveness. He *boldly* corrected others when they mistook His identity. He *boldly* refuted Satan regarding His identity. He was His own Audience of One. And He drowned out every other voice. Every thief who would compromise the truth of who He was.

He defined Himself. He longs to define you.

Let His be the solitary voice that declares your worth.

And then follow His footsteps by *boldly* correcting any attack of the enemy that fuels a false belief about who you really are. *Boldly* refute the lies. *It's time to stop the theft of your identity* and gain stability by rescuing your significance as the person you were created to be. It's time to disarm the thief and take back the security that never should have been stolen.

God loves you with an outlandish, radical love. And I promise you, that love He has for you is beyond anything you've ever experienced in this life. Allow His love to cover you, to wash over you, to heal you, to retrain your thoughts about yourself, to stabilize your emotions, and to influence your decisions. As you accept that covering of love and seek Him for insight regarding your worth, you will find healing for your mind and your emotions.

A radical dependence on Him and acceptance of your true identity (by His definition) will result in stability. This dependence and acceptance will starve your vulnerability to make comparisons and change how you judge your appearance. They will change how you define success and failure. They will change your drive for approval or your fear of rejection. They will change the weight of your life experiences and traumas. They will change your attachment to your roles and responsibilities. They will change the impact your background and origin have on your life.

A radical dependence on Him will also eliminate the unnecessary problems that have been created by false beliefs. You can experience freedom from depression, from an obsession with body image, from anger and panic, from jealousy, from shame and feelings of inadequacy, from being needy or self-absorbed, from social anxiety, from self-consciousness and sensitivity, from destructive relationships and codependency, and from addictions.

Freedom to live. To thrive. To grow. To love yourself as God loves you.

Genuinely healed self-worth and confident assurance of your significance change *everything*!

Let Him rescue you. Let Him transform your identity. And then He will transform your entire life.

During stressful times, you may be triggered back into your old way of thinking. When you are at your weakest, the enemy will likely assault you with old, familiar lies and false accusations. Residual struggles with insecurity will remain this side of eternity. But persist. Boldly fight for your freedom. And allow God to rescue you for as many times as you need to be rescued. Because, yes, you are worth the fight. And you are worthy of freedom— *freedom from insecurity!*

Thanks for joining me on this journey. If you have found some healing here, go share these truths with a Christian sister. Many are in need of rescue.

Donna

Appendix

Scripture Truths for a Secure Identity

U se this prayer and these Scriptures as tools for building your case against the enemy. Remember, both repetition and meditation are required for replacing the false beliefs that may be deeply ingrained in you. Review these truths daily for at least sixty days after you read this book. Put them in your own words and embrace the *real* you. The *free* you.

God, thank You for this freeing journey. I choose to agree with You, about both who You are and who I am. I will guard my heart from the enemy's lies and the lies born from my past, my interactions with others, my successes or failures, and my appearance. You are now my Audience of One, and You are more than worthy of that role. I will no longer be a slave to my insecurities. From this point forward, I will accept Your truths about my identity. I will think on truth, I will meditate on truth, and I will wage war against any false charge against me. I embrace Your purposes for my life. Thank You for allowing me to be living light, that others may also find freedom.

When you experience rejection:

I am His child (John 1:12).

I am a friend of Jesus (John 15:5).

I am choosing God to be my Audience of One. He didn't reject me (Rom. 5:8).

I am a fellow heir with Christ (Rom. 8:17).

I am a part of the body of Christ (Rom. 12:4–5).

I am accepted by Christ (Rom. 15:7).

I am chosen (Eph. 1:4).

I am adopted into His family (Eph. 1:5).

I am choosing relationships that sharpen me and bring healing (Prov. 27:17).

When you feel unworthy or not good enough:

I am not going to be deceived by my emotions. I will rely on truth (Jer. 17:9).

I am delighted in. He rejoices over me with singing (Zeph. 3:17).

I am seeing myself with healthy eyes (Matt. 6:22–24).

I am bought with a price. I belong to God (1 Cor. 6:19–20).

I am His masterpiece, His workmanship, His handiwork (Eph. 2:10).

I am not allowing my heart to condemn me (1 John 3:20).

When you feel shame or you regret the past:

I am not relying on my own understanding about myself. I choose truth (Prov. 3:5–6).

I will forget my shame (Isa. 54:4).

I am forgiven (Rom. 3:24).

I am not condemned (Rom. 8:1–2).

I am a new person in Christ. The old person is gone (2 Cor. 5:17).

I am holy and blameless in His sight (Eph. 1:4).

I am redeemed (Col. 1:14).

I refuse to be identified by my past (Heb. 11:24–28).

When you feel all alone:

I am with God (Zeph. 3:17).

I am the temple of the Holy Spirit (1 Cor. 6:19).

I am brought near to God and bought with a price (Eph. 2:13).

I belong to Christ Jesus (Eph. 3:6).

When you are overwhelmed:

I am made strong with God's power, even when I feel weak (2 Cor. 12:9–10).

I am filled with peace. He is my peace (Eph. 2:14).

I am able to approach God with freedom and confidence (Eph. 3:12).

I am empowered with strength through His Spirit (Eph. 3:16).

I am able to do all things through Christ who strengthens me (Phil. 4:13).

I am not given a spirit of fear. I am given power, love, and a sound mind (2 Tim. 1:7).

When you feel broken:

I am fearfully and wonderfully made (Ps. 139:13–14).

I have always been known by God (Jer. 1:5).

I am united with Christ (Eph. 1:3).

I am choosing to think on truth (Phil. 4:8).

I am complete in Christ (Col. 2:10).

When you fear the future:

I have the help and protection of God (Ps. 121).

I am assured that all things will work together for good (Rom. 8:28).

I am a conqueror (Rom. 8:35, 37).

I am being transformed, by the renewing of my mind (Rom. 12:2).

I am prepared to wage war against the enemy (Eph. 6:12–18).

I am confident that God will finish what He started in me (Phil. 1:6).

I am cared for (Phil. 4:19).

I am given grace and mercy when I need it (Heb. 4:16).

I am resisting Satan (James 4:7).

When you need to be reminded that you are free:

I am living with purpose (Esther 4:14).

I am forgetting the past. God is doing something new in me (Isa. 43:18).

I am new, with a new name (Isa. 62:2).

I am shining a light, so that others may also be encouraged (Matt. 5:14–16).

I am holding on to truth, and it is setting me free (John 7:31–32).

I am thinking with genuine humility and no longer from false humility (Rom. 12:3).

I am a new creature in Christ (2 Cor. 5:17).

I am set free in Christ. I will stand firm, and no longer be burdened by lies (Gal. 5:1).

I am alive with Christ (Eph. 2:4–5).

I am living light (Phil. 2:15).

Notes

Introduction

1. *Merriam-Webster*, s.v. "identity crisis," accessed February 19, 2018, https://www.merriam-webster.com/dictionary/identity%20crisis.

Chapter 1 Appearance and Comparisons

1. Neil Katz, "Life-Size Barbie's Shocking Dimensions: Would She Be Anorexic?" CBS News, April 21, 2011, http://www.cbsnews.com/news/life-size-barbies-shocking-dimensions-photo-would-she-be-anorexic/.

Chapter 4 Life Experiences and Trauma

1. Sarah Reiland and Dean Lauterbach, "Effects of Trauma and Religiosity on Self-Esteem," *Psychological Reports* 102, no 3, (2008): 779–90.

Chapter 8 Mental

1. Donna Gibbs, *Becoming Resilient: How to Move through Suffering and Come Back Stronger* (Grand Rapids: Revell, 2017), 53–54.
2. Robert McGee, *Search for Significance: Seeing Your True Worth through God's Eyes* (Houston: Rapha Publishing, 1990), 168.
3. Gibbs, *Becoming Resilient*, 106.

Chapter 9 Emotional

1. Tanya Lewis, "How Men's Brains Are Wired Differently than Women's," *LiveScience*, December 2, 2013, http://www.livescience.com/41619-male-female-brains-wired-differently.html.

2. Gregory L. Jantz, PhD, "Brain Differences between Genders," *Psychology Today*, February 17, 2014, https://www.psychologytoday.com/blog/hope-relationships/201402/brain-differences-between-genders.

Chapter 11 Developmental

1. Jane Anderson, "The Impact of Family Structure on the Health of Children: Effects of Divorce," *The Linacre Quarterly*, November 2014, https://www.ncbi.nlm.nih.gov/pmc/articles/PMC4240051/.

Chapter 13 Audience of One

1. Turron Davenport, "Eagles Marcus Smith Explains What's behind AO1 Cleats by Carson Wentz," EaglesWire, December 2, 2016, http://theeagleswire.usatoday.com/2016/12/02/eagles-marcus-smith-explains-whats-behind-ao1-cleats-by-carson-wentz/.

Donna Gibbs graduated from North Carolina State University in 1993 with a BA in psychology. In 1997, she earned an MS in community counseling from Western Carolina University. She earned a PhD in Christian counseling and psychology from Louisiana Baptist University in 2007. She is a Licensed Professional Counselor Supervisor, a National Certified Counselor, a Board Certified Professional Christian Counselor, and an adjunct online professor of counseling for Fruitland Bible Institute. She is on the professional referral networks for Focus on the Family, Crisis Care Network, and Finding Balance (an online eating disorder recovery resource). She is a professional provider for Samaritan's Purse and a member of the American Association of Christian Counselors (AACC).

In partnership with a colleague, Donna developed Summit Wellness Centers in 2018 in an effort to provide more accessible resources to various organizations and churches in her region. Previously, she directed A Clear Word Counseling Center (CWCC), which became a thriving resource for those experiencing emotional or relationship struggles. Donna has authored various books and is commonly featured on radio broadcasts across America. Donna has been married to her husband, Mark, for nearly twenty-five years and has four active and fun-loving boys.

Donna frequently enjoys speaking and training engagements and would be honored to come to your church or organization to share a word of instruction or encouragement. She welcomes you to follow her Facebook page and weekly blog at: https://www.facebook.com/DonnaGibbsResilience and www.summitwellnesscenters.com.

CONNECT WITH DONNA ONLINE AT

SummitWellnessCenters.com

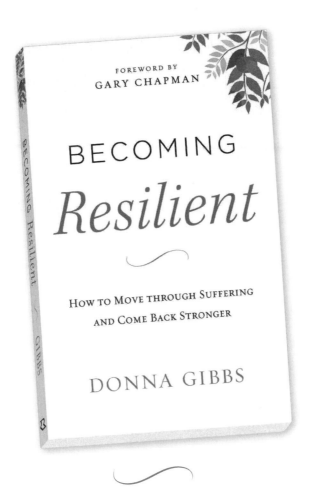